SPSS MAN

FOR

HOWELL'S

FUNDAMENTAL STATISTICS
FOR THE BEHAVIORAL SCIENCES

Fifth Edition

Esther M. Leerkes
The University of Vermont

THOMSON

BROOKS/COLE

Australia • Canada • Mexico • Singapore • Spain • United Kingdom • United States

Printed in Canada
1 2 3 4 5 6 7 07 06 05 04 03

Printer: Transcontinental-Louiseville

ISBN: 0-534-39955-X

For more information about our products,
contact us at:
Thomson Learning Academic Resource Center
1-800-423-0563

For permission to use material from this text,
contact us by:
Phone: 1-800-730-2214
Fax: 1-800-731-2215
Web: http://www.thomsonrights.com

Cover: Theme Park Tidal Wave Pool. © Alex Maclean/ Photonica.

Asia
Thomson Learning
5 Shenton Way #01-01
UIC Building
Singapore 068808

Australia/ New Zealand
Thomson Learning
102 Dodds Street
South Street
Southbank, Victoria 3006
Australia

Canada
Nelson
1120 Birchmount Road
Toronto, Ontario M1K 5G4
Canada

Europe/Middle East/South Africa
Thomson Learning
High Holborn House
50/51 Bedford Row
London WC1R 4LR
United Kingdom

Latin America
Thomson Learning
Seneca, 53
Colonia Polanco
11560 Mexico D.F.
Mexico

Spain/ Portugal
Paraninfo
Calle/Magallanes, 25
28015 Madrid, Spain

CONTENTS

Preface

This manual is intended to accompany David Howell's Fundamental Statistics for the Social Sciences, 5th Edition, hereafter referred to as the textbook. Most of the examples used in this manual are drawn from the textbook. This manual is not intended to be an all-encompassing overview of SPSS. It is intended to illustrate the use of SPSS to conduct procedures covered in the textbook.

This manual includes hands-on activities in every chapter intended to increase your knowledge of SPSS. Simply reading this manual without attempting the activities is unlikely to increase your comfort with SPSS. You should follow the instructions in SPSS while reading the manual. Pictures of the dialog boxes you will encounter are included in this manual, but they are relatively small. They are included to reassure you that you are in the right place in SPSS. You should be able to read the specific content from your computer screen. The hands-on activities build on one another, so you should perform the activities in the order presented to maximize your learning. ✔ This check mark is used to denote specific steps that should be followed for the hands-on activities. Important commands and checkboxes are boldfaced in the instructions (e.g., click **Continue**, select **Save standardized values**). These instructions were written based on the assumption that readers have a working knowledge of Windows based programs. Solutions to these activities appear in the body of this manual.

Every chapter concludes with exercises, most of which offer an additional opportunity to practice procedures outlined in the hands-on activities. Completing these exercises independently will greatly improve your comfort with SPSS. An answer key is included at the end of this manual.

The accompanying CD includes the files needed for the hands-on activities and the exercises. The CD is read only, so you will need to save new files and files that you alter to other sources.

This manual was designed around SPSS version 10.1. You may be using anything from Version 9 to 11.5. These versions are very similar, and the same instructions should hold.

1: Introduction to SPSS

Objectives

- ◆ Learn about SPSS
- ◆ Open SPSS
- ◆ Review the layout of SPSS
- ◆ Become familiar with Menus and Icons
- ◆ Exit SPSS

What is SPSS?

SPSS is a Windows based program that can be sued to perform data entry and analysis and to create tables and graphs. SPSS is capable of handling large amounts of data and can perform all of the analyses covered in the textbook and more. SPSS is commonly used in the Social Sciences and in the Business world, so familiarity with this program should serve you well in the future.

Opening SPSS

Depending on how the computer you are working on is structured, you can open SPSS in one of two ways.

1. If there is an SPSS shortcut like this on the desktop, simply put the cursor on it and double click the left mouse button.

2. Click the left mouse button on the button on your screen, then put your cursor on **Programs** or **All Programs** and left click the mouse. Select **SPSS 10.1 for Windows** by clicking the left mouse button. Either approach will launch the program.

✔ Use one of these approaches to open SPSS yourself.

You will see a screen that looks like the image that follows. The dialog box that appears offers choices of running the tutorial, typing in data, running queries, or opening an existing data source. The window behind this is the Data Editor window, which is used to display the data from whatever file you are using. You could select any one of the options on the start-up dialog box and click OK, or you could simply hit Cancel. If you hit Cancel, you can either enter new data in the blank Data Editor or you could open an existing file using the File menu bar as explained later.

✓ Click **Cancel**, and we'll get acquainted with the layout of SPSS.

Layout of SPSS

The *Data Editor* window has two views that can be selected from the lower left hand side of the screen. *Data View* is where you see the data you are using. *Variable View* is where you can specify the format of your data when you are creating a file or where you can check the format of a pre-existing file. The data in the *Data Editor* is saved in a file with the extension .sav.

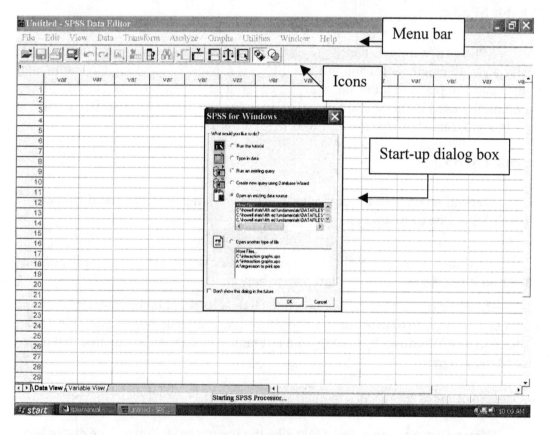

The other most commonly used SPSS window is the *SPSS Viewer* window which displays the output from any analyses that have been run and any error messages. Information from the Output Viewer is saved in a file with the extension .spo. Let's open an output file and look at it.

✔ On the **File** menu, click **Open** and select **Output**. Select *Appendix D output.spo* from your CD drive. Click **Ok**. The following will appear. The left hand side is an outline of all of the output in the file. The right side is the actual output. To shrink or enlarge either side put your cursor on the line that divides them. When the double headed arrow appears, hold the left mouse button and move the line in either direction. Release the button and the size will be adjusted.

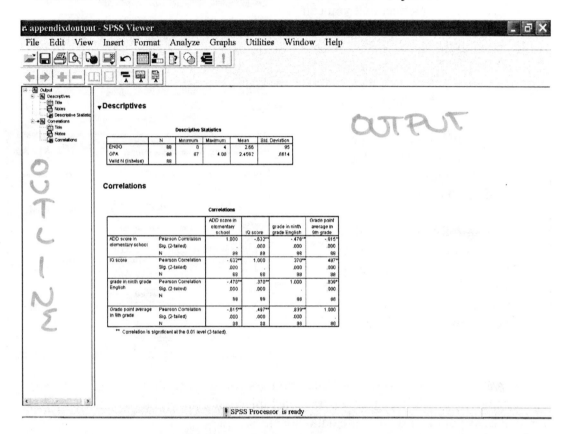

Finally, there is the *Syntax* window which displays the command language used to run various operations. Typically, you will simply use the dialog boxes to set up commands, and would not see the Syntax window. The Syntax window would be activated if you pasted the commands from the dialog box to it, or if you wrote you own syntax--something we will not focus on here. Syntax files end in the extension .sps.

SPSS Menus and Icons

Now, let's review the menus and icons.

3

✓ Review the options listed under each menu on the Menu Bar by clicking them one at a time. Follow along with the below descriptions.

File includes all of the options you typically use in other programs, such as open, save, exit. Notice, that you can open or create new files of multiple types as illustrated to the right.

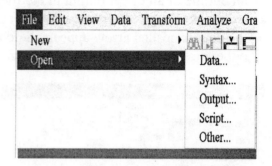

Edit includes the typical cut, copy, and paste commands, and allows you to specify various options for displaying data and output.

✓ Click on **Options**, and you will see the dialog box to the left. You can use this to format the data, output, charts, etc. These choices are rather overwhelming, and you can simply take the default options for now.

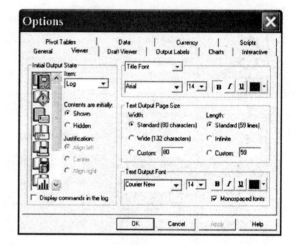

View allows you to select which toolbars you want to show, select font size, add or remove the gridlines that separate each piece of data, and to select whether or not to display your raw data or the data labels.

Data allows you to select several options ranging from displaying data that is sorted by a specific variable to selecting certain cases for subsequent analyses.

Transform includes several options to change current variables. For example, you can change continuous variables to categorical variables, change scores into rank scores, add a constant to variables, etc.

Analyze includes all of the commands to carry out statistical analyses and to calculate descriptive statistics. Much of this book will focus on using commands located in this menu.

4

Graphs includes the commands to create various types of graphs including box plots, histograms, line graphs, and bar charts.

Utilities allows you to list file information which is a list of all variables, there labels, values, locations in the data file, and type.

Window can be used to select which window you want to view (i.e., Data Editor, Output Viewer, or Syntax). Since we have a data file and an output file open, let's try this.

✔ Select **Window/Data Editor**. Then select **Window/SPSS Viewer**.

Help has many useful options including a link to the SPSS homepage, a statistics coach, and a syntax guide. Using **Topics**, you can use the **Index** option to type in any key word and get a list of options, or you can view the categories and subcategories available under contents. This is an excellent tool and can be used to troubleshoot most problems.

The Icons directly under the Menu bar provide shortcuts to many common commands that are available in specific menus. Take a moment to review these as well.

✔ Place your cursor over the **Icons** for a few seconds, and a description of the underlying command will appear. For example, this icon ▣ is the shortcut for Save. Review the others yourself.

In the chapters that follow, we will review many specific functions available through these Menus and Icons, but it is important that you take a few moments to familiarize yourself with the layout and options before beginning.

Exiting SPSS

To close SPSS, you can either left click on the close button ☒ located on the upper right hand corner of the screen or select **Exit** from the **File** menu.

✔ Choose one of these approaches, and exit SPSS.

A dialog box like the one that follows will appear for every open window asking you if you want to save it before exiting. You almost always want to save data files.

Output files may be large, so you should ask yourself if you need to save them or if you simply want to print them.

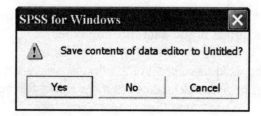

✔ Click **No** for each dialog box since we do not have any new files or changed files to save.

Exercises

1. Look up "ANOVA" in **Help/Help topics**. What kind of information did you find?

2. Look up "compare groups for significant differences" in **Help/ Statistics Coach**. What did you learn?

3. Open *Appenidx D.sav*. In the Data Viewer click **Grid Lines** in the **View** menu and note what happens.

4. While in the Data Viewer for *Appenidx D.sav*, click **Font** in the **View** menu and select the font style and size of your choice.

5. Using **Edit/Options/General**, under **Variable List** select **Display Labels** and **File**. In future this means that SPSS will list the variables in the order they appear in the file using the variable labels rather than variable names. As you are analyzing data in future exercises try to notice whether or not you like this option. If not, change it.

2: Entering Data

Objectives

- ◆ Understand the logic of data files
- ◆ Create data files and enter data
- ◆ Insert cases and variables
- ◆ Merge data files (optional)
- ◆ Read data into SPSS from other sources

The Logic of Data Files

Each row typically represents the data from 1 case, whether that be a person, animal, or object. Each column represents a different variable. A cell refers to the juncture of a specific row and column. For example, the first empty cell in the right hand corner would include the data for case 1, variable 1.

Entering Data

✔ Open SPSS and follow along as your read this description.

To enter data, you could simply begin typing information into each cell. If you did so, SPSS would give each column a generic label such as var00001. Clearly this is not desirable because you would have no way of identifying what var00001 meant later on, unless you have a superior memory. Instead, we want to specify names for our variables. To do this, you can either double left click on a any column head, this will automatically take you to the Variable View. Alternatively, you can simply click on Variable View on the bottom left hand corner of your screen.

The first column of variable view is **Name**. The default length for variable names is 8 characters. It is very important that you give your variables names that make intuitive sense. This is easy if words under 8 characters come to mind, if not you will need to use thoughtful abbreviations. For example, if I had depression data that was collected at intake, and 1 month, 6 months, and 1 year post intervention, I would name those variables depress0 or depresin (i.e., in for intake), depress1, depress6, and depres12. SPSS also has preferences for variable names. For example, a number cannot begin a variable name (e.g., 12depres would not be a valid name). Error messages will appear if you have selected a name that is "illegal" to SPSS. The rules for variable names appear below. They can be found by typing "variable names" in the **Index** option under **Help** and then selecting rules from the list that appears.

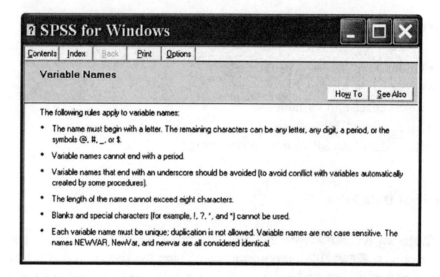

Next, you can select the **Type** of variable. Left click on the cell you want to change, then left click on the gray box that appears. The dialog box to the right appears. The most commonly used types of data include numeric, date, and string. For numeric data, width and decimal places refer to the number of characters and decimal places that will be displayed in the Data Editor window.

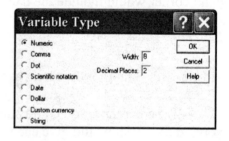

If you entered a value with 3 decimal places, SPSS would save that value, but would only display the value to 2 decimal places.

String variables are those that consist of text. For example, you could type male and female if gender were a variable of interest. It is important to note that SPSS is case sensitive meaning that "female" and "Female" would not be viewed as the same category. Misspellings are also problematic with string data (e.g., "femal" would not be recognized as the intended "female"). For these reasons, it is advantageous to use numbers to represent common categories, and then supply labels for those levels as discussed below.

✔ Click on **Date** to see the variety of available formats. Then, click **Cancel**.

The next columns are for **Width** and **Decimals**. You could have set this while specifying your variable type, or you can specify them in these columns. The default for width is 8 characters and the default for decimals is 2. To change this, left click the cell, and up and down arrows will appear, as illustrated below. Left click the up arrow if you want to increase the number, click the down arrow to decrease the value. Alternatively, you can simply type the desired value in the cell.

	Name	Type	Width	Click here to change the width	Missing
1	depresin	Numeric	8		one

The next column is **Label**. This is a very nice feature that allows you to provide more information about the variable than you could fit in the 8 character variable name. For example, I could type "Depression assessed at intake" for the example used above. When you hold your cursor over a variable name in the Data View, the full label will appear. This is very useful when you need a quick reminder. An example of this feature is below.

Since labels are so much more detailed than variable names, we can specify that SPSS label variables this way in dialog boxes and output. Let's do this.

✔ Click **Edit/Options/Output Labels** and specify labels for each of the options. Then click **Ok**.

The next column is **Values**. This allows you to assign variable labels. You will typically use this option for categorical variables. For example, we may want the number 1 to represent males and the number 2 to represent females when we enter data on gender. Let's try this.

✔ Type gender in the first **Name** column.

✔ Scroll over to the **Values** column and left click. Then, left click on the gray box that appears on the right hand side of the cell. The Value Labels dialog box will appear.

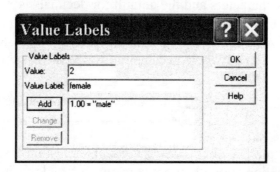

✔ Type the numeric value where it says **Value**, then type the **Value Label** or text to explain what it means. Click **Add**. Do this for males and females. When you are done, click **Ok**.

Of the remaining columns, you are most likely to use **Align**, which allows you to specify how the data will appear in the cells. Your choices are left justified, right justified, or centered. This is simply a matter of personal preference.

After you have completed specifying your variables, you can click on Data View and begin entering your data. Put your cursor on the cell in which you want to enter data. Type the value. If you hit Enter the cursor will move to the cell under the one you just filled. You can also use the arrow keys to move to the next cell in any given direction. Typically, you will either enter all of the values in one column by going down or you will enter all of the variables in a row going from left to right.

Let's try this together.

✔ On your disk, **Open** *depression scores.sav*. SPSS will ask you if you want to save the file with the gender variable. Click **No**. Then, SPSS will open *depression scores*. As you can see, variables have been named and labeled, but the data have not been entered.

✔ Enter the following data in the Variable View window. Pay attention to your own preferences for data entry (i.e., using the arrows or enter, going down or across).

✔ When you are done, click **Save As**, and save the file on a floppy disk or your hardrive. You cannot save it on this CD because it is read-only. Do not close the file. We will continue to use it as an example.

ID	depressin	depress1	depress6	depres12
1	30.000	25.00	23.00	20.00
2	32.000	30.00	30.00	28.00
3	35.000	35.00	35.00	40.00
4	45.000	42.00	40.00	35.00
5	45.000	45.00	38.00	40.00
6	25.000	25.00	20.00	20.00
7	60.000	45.00	30.00	40.00
8	55.000	50.00	40.00	35.00
9	40.000	40.00	35.00	30.00
11	37.000	30.00	25.00	20.00
12	30.000	25.00	22.00	20.00

Inserting a Variable

After specifying the types of variables for the depression data, I realized I forgot to include a column for ID number. Typically, I like ID to be the first variable in my data file. I can add this in one of two ways.

1. In Variable View, highlight the first row and then click **Insert Variable** on the **Data** menu. This will place a new variable before the selected variable.

2. In Data View, highlight the first variable column and then click the **Insert Variable** icon. This will also place a new variable column at the beginning of the file.

✔ Use one of the approaches above to insert the new variable at the beginning of the file.

✔ Name the variable ID, and label it as participant identification number.

✔ Enter the ID data that appeared on the previous page.

✔ Click **Save**, and leave the file open.

11

Inserting a Case

As you can see, the data for ID 10 is missing. I found the missing data and want to enter it in the file. I'd like my data to be in order by ID number, so I want to insert a case between the person with ID 9 and ID 11. To do so, I can highlight the row for the case with ID 11, and either:

1. click on **Insert Case** on the **Data** menu or

2. click on the **Insert Case** icon . In either case, a blank row will appear before the highlighted case. Try it yourself.

✔ Insert a case for ID 10 using one of the above approaches.

✔ Enter the following data:10, 38, 35, 35 for ID, depresin, depress1, depress6, and depres12 respectively.

✔ Check the accuracy of your data entry, then click **Save**.

Merging Files

NOTE: This section is rather advanced and may be considered optional.

Adding Cases. Sometimes data that are related may be in different files that you would like to combine or merge. For example, in a research methods class, every student may collect and then enter data in their own data file. Then, the instructor might want to put all of their data into one file that includes more cases for data analysis. In this case, each file contains the same variables but different cases. To combine these files, have one of the data files open, then left click on **Merge Files** on the **Data** menu and select **Add Cases**. Then specify the file from which the new data will come and click **Open**. A dialog box will appear showing you which variables will appear in the new file. View it, and if all seems in order, click OK. The two files will be merged. This is fairly simple. See if you can do it yourself in Exercise 3 at the end of this chapter.

Adding Variables. In other cases, you might have different data on the same cases or participants in different files. For example, I may have recorded the demographic information from the participants in my depression study in one file and the depression data in another file. I may want to put them together because I'd like to see if demographic variables, like socioeconomic status or gender are related to depression. In this case, you need to be sure the variables on the same participants end up in the correct row, that is, you want to match the cases. In this case, we will use ID to match cases. SPSS requires that the files you merge be in ascending order by the matching variable. So, in both files, ID must start at 1. You can set this up by sorting cases as discussed above. Then, make sure one of the files is open. Since this procedure is more complicated, let's try this one together.

✔ Open *depression scores.sav* from wherever you just saved it.

✔ Check to see if the cases are in ascending order by ID. They should be since we just entered them that way.

✔ Now, open *depression demographics.sav* from this CD. These data are not in order by ID. To fix this, click **Sort Cases** under the **Data** menu.

✔ In the dialog box, select participant identification number and move it into the **Sort by** box by clicking the arrow. Make sure **Ascending** is selected for **Sort Order**. Then click **Ok**.

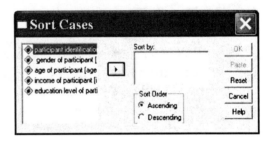

✔ While the demographic file is still open, click on **Merge Files** in the **Data** menu, and select **Add Variables**.

✔ The next dialog box will ask you to indicate which file the new variables are coming from. Select *depression scores.sav* and click **Ok**. The following dialog box will appear.

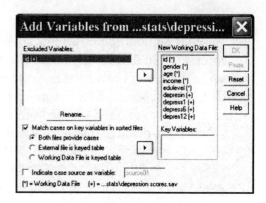

✓ Select **Match cases on key variable in sorted files**, then highlight id under excluded variables, then click the arrow to move id to **Key Variables**. Click **Ok**.

✓ A dialog box will appear, reminding you that the files must be sorted. Click **Ok**, and the files will be merged. You may want to do a **Save As** and give the merged file a new name like *depression complete.sav* to help you remember what is in it. Remember, you have to save it to a source other than this CD.

Reading Data In From Other Sources

SPSS can also recognize data from several other sources. For example, you can open data from Microsoft EXCEL in SPSS or you can get SPSS to read data entered in a text file. This is an attractive option, particularly if you do not have your own version of SPSS. It allows you to enter data in other more common programs, save them to disk, and simply open them when you have the opportunity to use a PC that has SPSS on it. Let's try some examples.

Opening data from EXCEL. The complete depression data is also on your disk in a file named *complete depression.xls* (xls is the extension for Excel data files). Take a moment to open this file in Excel and look it over. You will see it looks just like the file we just created except that the variable names are different because they are longer. Since we know SPSS only allows variable names with 8 characters, we'll need to change these names. If we don't SPSS will truncate them to 8 characters. This is a problem in this case because all 4 depression variables start with the same 8 characters. SPSS does not allow multiple variables to have the same name, so it would give the last 3 depression variables generic names like var7, var8, and var9 because they are the 7th, 8th, and 9th variables in the file. This is not desirable since we may not remember what they are supposed to represent. Essentially, if you plan to read Excel data into SPSS, you should follow all of the variable name guidelines specified by SPSS (e.g., character length, no numbers beginning a name, etc). Specific instructions follow.

✓ In Microsoft Excel, **Open** *complete depression.xls* from the **File** menu.

✔ Rename the variables in Excel to include eight characters. To do so, simply put your cursor in the cell containing the variable name and start typing, then hit the right arrow to move to the next cell. When you are done, **Save** your changes and close the file because SPSS cannot read the file if it is open in another program.

✔ In SPSS, select **Read Text Data** from the **File** menu.

✔ A dialog box will appear. Under **Files of type**, select **Excel**. Under **Look in** select your CDdrive. *Depression complete.xls* should appear. Select it and click **Open**. The following dialog box will appear.

✔ Select **Read variable names from the first row of data**, because that is where the names appear in the Excel file. Then, click **Ok**. Check out your new file in SPSS. How does it look? There is no need to save this file since it contains the same information as *depression complete.sav*.

The downside is the new data file does not include variable labels or values, so you would need to add them. You should also make sure that SPSS has identified the variables as the correct type.

Text Data. Now, let's try an example with text data. A text data file can be created in any word processing program or in Notepad or any other text editor. Just be sure to save the file with the .txt or .dat file extension. SPSS can recognize text data in several formats. Let's begin with the simplest example. I have collected data from 11 people and typed it in the following format (this is a sample, not the whole file).

012345	The first two digits are the ID number. The next digit is
021123	gender. Digits 4, 5, and 6 are the responses to the first 3
031234	questions on a survey. No characters or spaces separate the
042345	variables. The data are on your disk in *simpletextdata.txt*

✔ In the SPSS **File** menu, click **Read text data**. There is no need to save the previous file, so you can click **No**.

✔ Select *simple text data* under **Files of type Text** and click **Open**.

- ✔ In the next dialog box, click **No** for "Does your text file have a predefined format" and click **Next**.

- ✔ In the next dialog box, select **Fixed width** under "How are your variables arranged," then select **No** for "Are variable names included in the top of your file." Then click **Next**.

- ✔ In the next dialog box, indicate that the data starts on line **1**, **1** line represents a case, and you want to import **all cases**, then click **Next**. The following dialog box will appear. We need to tell SPSS where to insert breaks for variables.

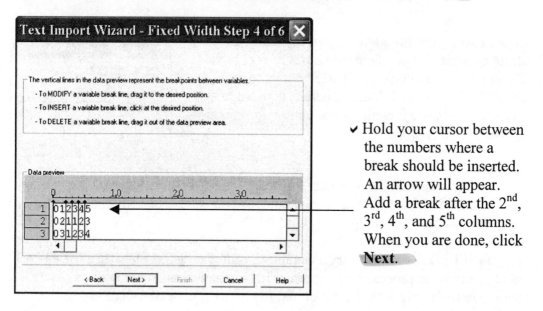

- ✔ Hold your cursor between the numbers where a break should be inserted. An arrow will appear. Add a break after the 2nd, 3rd, 4th, and 5th columns. When you are done, click **Next**.

- ✔ The next dialog box will show you a draft of what your new data file will look like. Notice, the variables will have generic names like v1, v2, etc. Then click **Next**.

- ✔ At the next dialog box, you can click **Finish** and your new data file will appear. You could then specify variable names, types, and labels as illustrated above.

Let's take one more example. This is based on the same data, but this time the text file is tab delimitated (a tab was inserted between each variable) and has variable names at the top. Below, is an example of the first two lines of from this text file.

```
ID      GenderQ1    Q2    Q3
01      2      3     4     5
```

- ✔ On the **File** menu, click **Read text data**.

- ✔ Select *tab text data* under **Files of type Text**, then click **Open**.

- ✔ On the next dialog box, you will see a draft that shows a box ☐ between each variable to represent the tabs. Are they in the right place? Select **No** for predefined format and then click **Next**.

- ✔ Select **Delimited** for file arrangement and **Yes** for variable names at the top of the file, then click **Next**.

- ✔ In the next dialog box, indicate that the data starts on line **1, 1** line represents a case, and you want to import **all cases**, then click **Next**.

- ✔ In the next dialog box, check **Tab** as the type of delimiter and then click **Next**.

- ✔ You will see a draft of your data file. Review it, and then click **Next**.

- ✔ Click **Finish** at the next dialog box and your new data file will appear.

One difference between these two examples, is the second included the variable names at the top of the file. This, in my opinion, is the better approach because it reduces the chance of making mistakes later in the process.

- ✔ **Exit** SPSS. There is no need to save the data file unless you want it for some reason.

This chapter included information about entering data and opening files of various types. This is an important part of the process because data entry errors contribute to inaccurate results. Further, good variable names and labels allow you to perform subsequent analyses more efficiently. Completing the following exercises will help you internalize these processes.

1. Open *RxTime.sav*. These are the data from Table 3.1 in your text. Label the variables as described in the textbook.

2. Read the data from Fig3-2.dat on the CD. These are the data on intrusive thoughts shown in Figure 3.2 of your text. These are raw data with variable names in the first line.

3. Review the following data. Then, create your own data file and enter the data. Be sure to include variable and value labels. Then open *Exercise 2.2.sav* on the CD which includes the same data. Note the similarities and differences between your file and the file on disk. Which do you prefer? Why?

Age	Gender	Average Hours of Sleep	Number of Classes Missed	Grade in Course
18	Male	Seven	0	A
18	Female	Four	1	C
17	Female	Six	2	B
19	Female	Ten	5	F
20	Male	Eight	2	B
21	Female	Seven and a half	3	C
23	Male	Nine	1	B
22	Male	Eight	2	A
18	Male	Six	3	D

4. Merge the following files from the disk using the add cases option: *merge1.sav* and *merge2.sav*.

5. Read the following text data file into SPSS: *text data exercise.txt*. Be sure to open the text file and notice the format before you proceed.

6. Read *read excel exercise.xls* into SPSS. Note any problems that arise and how you solved them.

3: Graphing Data

Objectives

- ◆ Create histograms, box plots, stem-and-leaf plots, bar graphs, scatterplots, and line graphs
- ◆ Edit graphs using the Chart Editor
- ◆ Use chart templates

SPSS has the capability to create many types of charts as can be seen by clicking on the **Graphs** menu bar. The options are illustrated to the right. Graphs can also be created by using options available in some dialog boxes for analyses. For example, histograms can be created from the Graphs menu or from **Analyze/ Descriptive Statistics/Frequencies**. In this chapter, we will focus on the Graphs menu. Additional options will be discussed throughout the book. One thing to focus on throughout this chapter is the various options for editing graphs.

We will begin with frequency distributions. Follow the steps as your read along.

Frequency Distributions

Frequency distributions plot the number of occurrences or counts for each value of a variable. Let's start by looking at the frequency of social problems from the data in Appendix D.

✔ **Open** *Appenidx D.sav.*

✓ Under **Graphs**, select **Bar.**

✓ At the next dialog box, select **Simple** and **Summaries for groups of cases**. Then click **Define**.

✓ In the next dialog box, select the social problems variable, and put it into **Category Axis** by using the arrow. Make sure **N of cases** (meaning number of cases) is selected for **Bars Represent**, then click **Ok**. The graph will appear in the Output Viewer window.

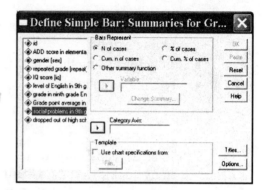

✓ To edit the graph, double click on it and the Chart Editor view will open. The Chart Editor has several Menu bars and Icons. Take a moment to review them by clicking on the menus and reading the commands that appear and putting your cursor over the icons and reading the descriptions that appear to the bottom left hand corner.

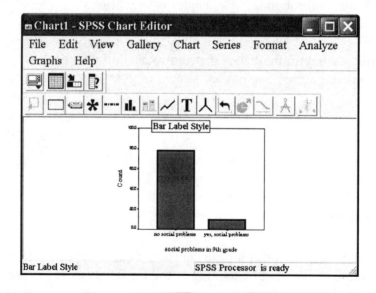

My chart displayed the value labels ("no social problems," and "yes, social problems") rather than the numbers 0 and 1 because we specified this earlier using

Edit/Options. To edit virtually anything on a chart, you can double click it and relevant dialog boxes will appear. Let's try it.

✔ Double click the labels under the bars, and a dialog box will appear.

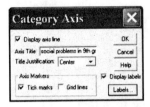

✔ To edit the title, click in the **Axis Title** box and begin typing. I like my labels to be capitalized, so I'll change it to "Social Problems in 9th Grade." I like titles to be centered, so don't change the title justification, but click on the arrow and look at the other options. Then, click **Labels** to change the bar or category labels. Another dialog box will appear.

✔ Notice, you can specify that SPSS show all value labels or intermittent labels. Select **All labels** since there are only 2 categories. If you had many categories, showing all labels might make things unreadable. Then, to edit the Label Text, highlight the label you want to change and then type in the box named Label. I will change the labels to a simple Yes and No since the variable label clarifies what Yes and No mean. Click change after you edit each one. Also, take a moment to view the options under Orientation. Select whichever one suits you. Then click **Continue**, which returns you to the previous dialog box, where you can click **OK**.

✔ I'd also like to change the Y axis to read Frequency rather than Count and to change the scale. To do this, double click on "Count" to activate the dialog box.

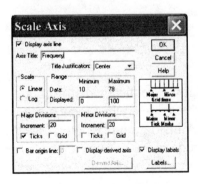

✔ Type Frequency in the **Axis Title** box, and select the type of **Title justification** you want. Then, in the box for **Major Divisions**, change it to 10 to alter the scale. Then click **Labels** and change the number of decimal places to 0. Click **Continue** and then **Ok**.

✔ To label the actual frequency value inside the bars, click on the **Bar Labels Style** Icon and select the style you like. Click **OK**.

21

- To change the color of the bars, single click the mouse when the cursor is over one of the bars, then click the **Color** Icon.

- Select **Fill**, then click on the color of your choice. Then, click **Apply**. If you don't like the colors, click **Edit** and create your own. Click **Apply** when done.

- To change the font of axis and category labels, click them once to select them, then use the Text icon to select different font styles and sizes as desired.

My final frequency distribution looks like this.

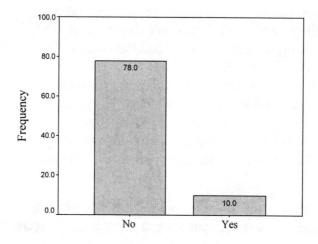

social problems in 9th grade

Histograms

As noted in the textbook, histograms are essentially a frequency distribution for ranges of values rather than individual values. These are ideal when there are several values and relatively low frequencies for each. A histogram is a perfect way to display the GPA data from Appendix D. Let's try it together.

- Select **Histogram** under **Graphs**.

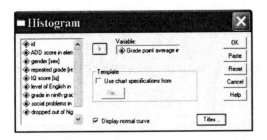

✔ Select grade point average for **Variable**. Check **Display the normal curve** if you want to see if the distributions is approximately normal. Then, click **Ok.**

✔ SPSS will select value ranges for you. If you want to change the ranges, double click on the values along the X axis. I like the way they are.

✔ On the dialog box that appears, select **Custom** under **Intervals** and then click **Define**. In the next box, indicate the number of intervals you would like and click **Continue**. Then, click **Ok.**

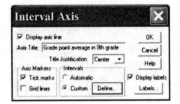

✔ Add a title for the Y axis as you did before. Double click the area, then type Frequency for the **Axis Title**, select the type of **Title justification** you want, and click **Ok**. The resulting graph will look like this.

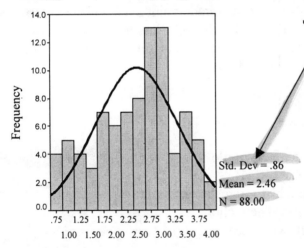

Grade point average in 9th grade

✔ SPSS includes descriptives as a default. If you don't want them on your histogram, double click in that area, unselect **Display Legend** in the dialog box that appears and click **Ok.**

Std. Dev = .86
Mean = 2.46
N = 88.00

✔ To add a title to your chart, click **Title** under the **Chart Menu**.

23

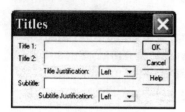

✔ Type in the title of your choice. **Title 1** and **Title 2** really mean line 1 and 2 of the title. select your **Title justification**, and click **Ok**. Notice that you could add a subtitle as well.

✔ Review your final histogram. Continue to edit it to fit your style (e.g., change the color, font, axes labels, etc).

Stem-and-Leaf Plot

As noted in the text, a stem-and-leaf plot is another type of histogram. This would be another appropriate way to display the GPA data. To create a stem and leaf plot, we will not use the Graphs menu. Rather, the stem-and-leaf plot is an option in the Analyze menu. Let's try one together.

✔ Select **Analyze/Descriptive Statistics/Explore**.

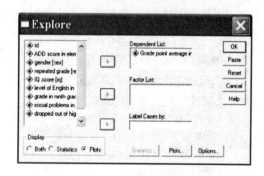

✔ Put Grade point average in the **Dependent list**. Select **Plots** under display since we are not calculating statistics yet, then click **Plots.**

✔ In the next dialog box, select **None** for **Boxplots**. Select **Stem-and-Leaf** under **Descriptives**. Note that you could create boxplots and histograms from here, although we won't right now. Then, click **Continue** and then **Ok**. The following stem-and-leaf plot will appear.

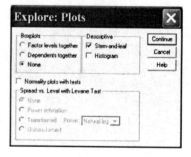

```
Grade point average in 9th grade Stem-and-Leaf Plot
    Frequency       Stem &   Leaf
      4.00          0 .   6667
      9.00          1 .   000002333
     10.00          1 .   5556677777
     14.00          2 .   00000022222234
     20.00          2 .   55555566667777777777
     18.00          3 .   000000000000022234
     11.00          3 .   55555577777
      2.00          4 .   00

Stem width:   1.00
Each leaf:    1 case(s)
```

✔ Notice the style of this chart is not as elegant as the others. To edit it, double click on it. This does not activate the Chart Editor since the stem-and-leaf plot is essentially text. It does activate the Output Editor though, which allows you to change font, alignment, color, etc. Edit the stem-and-leaf plot to suit your style.

Boxplots

Boxplots are useful to illustrate the dispersion of data. Let's create a boxplot together using the same data. We'll begin with a simple example.

✔ Select **Boxplot** under **Graphs.**

✔ Select **Simple** for style and click **Define**.

✔ Select grade point average for **Boxes Represent** and then click **Ok**. The resulting boxplot follows.

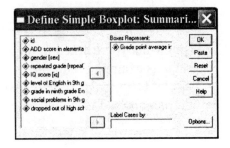

25

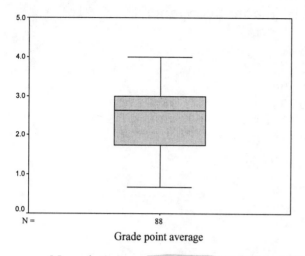

Grade point average

✔ Id like to change the scale on the Y axis to .5 units to make the median value more clear. Can you figure out how to do this on your own? [Double click the area, then change the **Major Divisions** as you did above.]

Now, let's try a more complicated boxplot. I'd like to see the boxplot of GPA in ninth grade for those who did and did not ultimately drop out of high school.

✔ Click on **Boxplot** in the **Graphs** menu.

✔ Select **Simple** and **Summaries for Groups of cases,** then click **Define**.

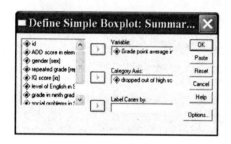

✔ Select grade point average as the **Variable** and dropped out of high school as the **Category Axis**. Then, click **Ok**. The resulting boxplot is below. Notice the difference between the two groups.

✔ Using what you learned in the previous examples, edit the boxplot to suit your style (e.g., edit the labels, change the color, change the scale, etc).

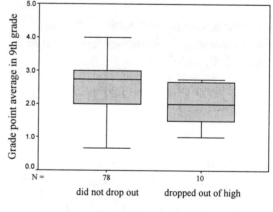

dropped out of high school

You can also create box plots for more than one variable. You would typically only do so if the variables are on a similar scale, which is not the case in the example we are using. This would be appropriate if we had GPA data from multiple points in time, for example. To create a box plot of this type, you would select **Simple** and **Summaries** of separate variables.

Bar Graphs

Another way to visually compare the data from different groups is a bar chart. Let's create one from the same example as above so we can compare them.

✔ Select **Bar** under **Graphs**.

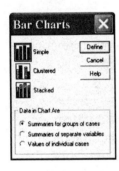

✔ Select **Simple** and **Summaries for groups of cases**, then click **Define**.

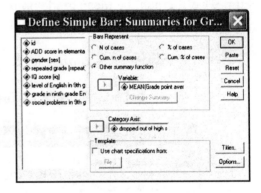

✔ Under **Bars Represent**, select **Other summary function**. Click **Change Summary**. Select **Mean of values,** but take a moment to review the other options, then click **Continue**. Put dropped out of high school in the **Category Axis**, then click **Ok**. The resulting graph follows.

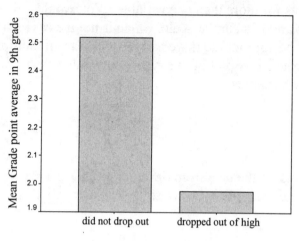

✔ Use what you learned above to edit the graph (e.g., change the text style, add a title, etc).

dropped out of high school

Notice the biggest difference between this and the boxplot on the previous page is that the boxplot gives you a sense of variability and central tendency. A bar graph of means does not illustrate variability.

Now, let's create a more complicated bar chart in which there are two independent variables. This is an ideal way to display main effects and interaction effects for factorial designs, which are discussed in Chapter 17 of the textbook. This time, we'll graph the mean grade point average based on both gender and whether or not the student ultimately dropped out.

✔ Select **Bar** from the **Graphs** menu.

✔ Select **Clustered** and **Summaries for groups of cases,** then click **Define.**

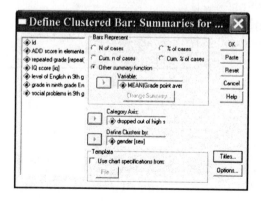

✔ Select **Bars Represent Other summary function**, and select GPA. Mean will be the default summary. Select dropped out of high school for the **Category Axis** and gender for the **Cluster.** Select **Titles** from this dialog box and type "GPA by Gender and Dropout Status." Then click **Ok.**

✔ Double click on the graph to activate the Chart Editor. When there are multiple independent variables, you have to decide which one should be displayed on the X- axis and which one should be used as the categories. Fortunately, you can shift them back and forth and decide which view is better. To do so, click **Transpose Data** in the **Series** menu as illustrated below.

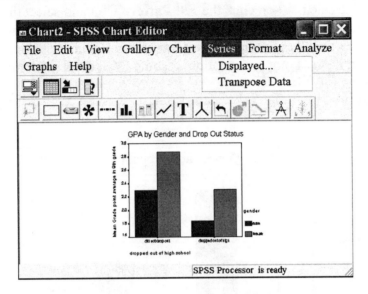

✔ Take a moment to view the new layout illustrated on the following page. Personally, I preferred the first graph with drop out status on the X-axis. So, click **Series/Transpose** again to return it to the first layout.

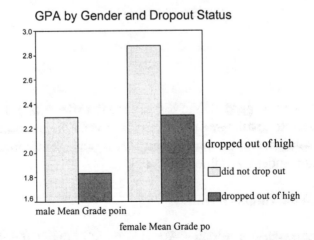

✔ Now, edit the labels and axes as you learned above so the graph makes sense and looks polished.

- It's very important that the gender groups are visually distinct from one another. Since I am printing to a black and white printer, I will use different shades of gray for each gender. [You can apply patterns to the bars to make them stand out from each other as well. To do so, click on one of the bars. You will see each of the related bars selected. Then click the **Fill Pattern** icon and select the fill of your choice and click **Apply**. The patterns will not stand out clearly when printed to a black and white printer, but they are a great option if you are planning to paste graphs into a Power Point presentation or some other color medium.] My final graph follows.

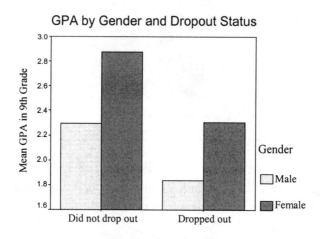

GPA by Gender and Dropout Status

Line Graphs

Line graphs can be used also to display mean differences. Line graphs are most commonly used to display mean differences over time or conditions. They can also be used to display mean differences between groups. Let's make a simple line graph with one independent variable.

- Select Line from the Graphs menu.

- Then select **Simple** and **Summaries for groups of cases**. Click **Define**.

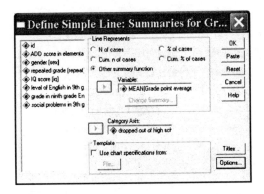

✔ Select **Other summary function** under **Line Represents**, then select GPA as the **Variable**. Mean is the default option. Select dropped out of school for the **Category Axis**. Then, click **Ok**.

✔ Double click on the graph to activate the Chart Editor. Then click on the **Line Style** icon. Change the style and weight of the line to suit your style and click **Apply**. My line graph follows.

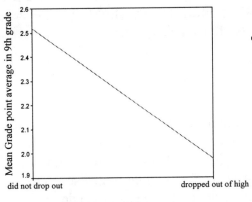

dropped out of high school

✔ Edit your graph (e.g., add a title, change the labels and scale, etc) as illustrated previously.

As with the bar graph, a line graph can also be used to display interactive effects. Let's create the same graph we did above illustrating mean GPA based on both gender and drop out status.

✔ Select **Line** from the **Graphs** menu.

✔ Select **Multiple** and **Summaries for groups of cases** and click **Define**.

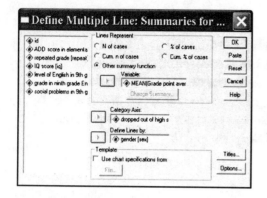

✔ Much like before, select **Other summary function**, Mean GPA for **Lines Represent**. Specify dropped out as the **Category Axis** and Gender for the **Lines**. Click **Titles**, name your graph, and click **Continue**. Then, click **Ok**.

✔ Double click the graph to activate the Chart Editor. As before, you can **Transpose the data** through the **Series** menu if you want, but I like the present layout.

✔ Now, I need the lines that represent gender to be distinct from one another. Click on a line, then click on the **Line Style** Icon. I am going to increase the weight of the line and make it dashed. Click **Apply**. I'd like the other line to be thicker as well. Click the other line, then the **Line Style** icon, select the heavier weight and click **Apply**.

✔ Edit the labels and axes as desired.

My final graph appears on the following page. Take a moment to interpret the graph and compare it to the bar graph we made of the same data. Which do you prefer? One thing that's nice about the line graph is that you can see the lines representing gender are parallel. In the language of factorial designs discussed in Chapter 17 of the textbook, I would guess there are main effects of gender and drop out status, but no interaction effect. Of course, we would need to calculate a Factorial ANOVA to be certain.

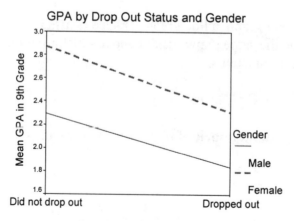

Scatterplots

Scatterplots are typically used to visualize relationships between continuous variables. In Appendix D, it makes sense to expect a positive association between IQ and GPA. Let's create this scatterplot together.

✓ Select **Scatter** under **Graphs**.

✓ Select **Simple** and click **Define**.

✓ Typically, the dependent variable is placed on the Y axis and the independent on the X axis. Although we cannot prove causality in this instance, theoretically it makes more sense that IQ contributes to GPA rather than the reverse. So, select grade point average for the **Y Axis** and IQ score for the **X Axis**, then click **Ok**. The scatterplot will appear.

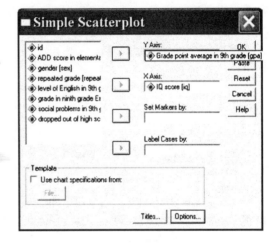

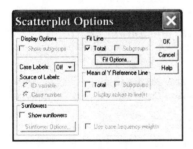

✓ Next, we can add a line of best fit to better illustrate the relationship. Double click on the chart to activate the Chart Editor. Then, select **Chart/Options**. Select **Total** under Fit Line. Then click **Fit Options** and select **Linear Regression**. Note the other options, then click **Continue**. Finally click **Ok**. The scatterplot follows.

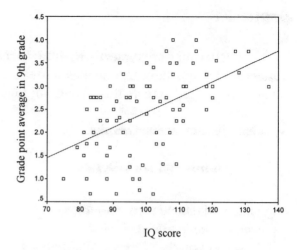

✔ Edit the graph to suit your style (e.g., change the font, colors, labels etc).

Based on the graph, it appears that GPA and IQ are positively correlated. Of course, we would calculate the correlation coefficient to confirm this statistically.

Chart Templates

If you do a lot of graphing and develop a style you particularly like, you can save it as a template for future graphs. This can save a lot of time editing.

✔ When you have created a graph you really like, in Chart Editor select **File/Save chart template** and save the file with a name that makes sense to you (e.g., interaction bar graph, simple bar graph, etc). The file extension for chart templates is .sct.

✔ The next time you are creating a similar graph, select **Use chart specification from,** then click **File** in the Define dialog box. Select the appropriate template, **click Open,** continue defining your graph and click **Ok.**

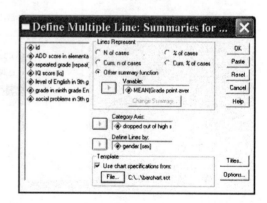

✓ **Exit** SPSS. There is no need to save the data file since we have not changed it. It is up to you to decide if you would like to save the output file for future reference. If you save it, make sure you give it a name that makes sense!

As you can see, SPSS is capable of creating many different chart types, and each type has many options. In addition, charts can be created from the Graphs menu and from the Analyze menu. Further, charts can be edited tremendously after they are created using the Chart Editor. I encourage you to complete the following exercises and try out several different options along the way-even those that were not covered in this chapter. This will increase your comfort with SPSS and clarify your own graphing preferences.

Exercises

Each of the following exercises is based on the data in *Appenidx D.sav*.

1. Create a histogram for ADDSC.

2. Create a boxplot for ADDSC. Then, create ADDSC boxplots for those with and without social problems. How would you describe the data?

3. Create a scatter plot illustrating the relationship between ADD symptoms and GPA. Include the line of best fit. Does there appear to be a relationship between these variables?

4. Create a bar chart to illustrate the mean GPA of students in each of the 3 types of English Classes. Do they appear to be similar or different?

5. Create a bar chart and a line graph illustrating mean differences in GPA based on both gender and level of English class. Do you think there are main effects of gender and type of class? Do you think there is an interaction effect? Which type of graph do you prefer and why?

4. Descriptive Statistics: Measures of Variability and Central Tendency

Objectives

- ♦ Calculate descriptive statistics for continuous and categorical data
- ♦ Edit output tables

Although measures of central tendency and variability were presented as separate chapters in the textbook, they are presented together here because they are options located in the same command windows in SPSS. Descriptive statistics are calculated using the Analyze menu. Most are calculated using either the Descriptives or Frequencies command under Descriptive Statistics. When calculating descriptives for more complex designs including more than one independent variable, you can also use the Means/ Compare Means or the Descriptive Statistics/ Crosstabs command which allow you to calculate descriptive statistics of subgroups.

It is always important to take a moment to think about the type of data you are using and what descriptive statistics will be most useful given the type. For continuous or measurement data, you typically report measures of central tendency and measures of variability. For categorical data (i.e., nominal data) you typically report the frequency of each value. Though you don't typically report the frequencies for continuous data, it is often useful to observe the frequency distributions or histograms of continuous distributions to note if they are normal or skewed.

Descriptive Statistics

Let's begin by calculating descriptive statistics for the data in Appendix D. In this data set, I think ADD symptoms, IQ score, English grade, and GPA are continuous variables. We'll calculate measures of central tendency and variability for each of these.

✔ **Open** *Appenidx D.sav.*

✔ In the **Analyze** menu, select **Descriptive Statistics** and then **Descriptives**.

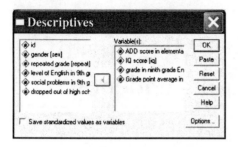

✔ Select each of the continuous variables by either double clicking them, which automatically puts them in the **Variable** list, highlight them one at a time by single clicking them and then clicking the arrow to shift them into the variable list, or by holding the control key down while highlighting all of the variables of interest and then shifting them into the variable list all at once by clicking the arrow. Then click **Options**.

✔ Select each of the measures you've been learning about (**Mean**, **Std. deviation**, **Variance**, **Range**, **Minimum** and **Maximum**). Then, select the **Display Order** you would prefer. This will determine the order they appear in for the resulting table. I like them in the order I indicated in the **Variable list**. Then click **Continue**.

✔ In the main descriptives dialog box, check the box that says **Save standardized values as variables**. SPSS will calculate z scores for each of the variables using the formula you learned about and append them to the end of your data file. Click **Ok**. The resulting output will look like this. Note that the variable labels are used rather than the variable names. Remember, we specified this as the default in Edit/Options/Output Labels.

Descriptive Statistics

	N	Range	Minimum	Maximum	Mean	Std. Deviation	Variance
ADD score in elementary school	88	59.0	26.0	85.0	52.602	12.422	154.311
IQ score	88	62.00	75.00	137.00	100.2614	12.9850	168.609
grade in ninth grade English	88	4	0	4	2.66	.95	.894
Grade point average in 9th grade	88	3.33	.67	4.00	2.4562	.8614	.742
Valid N (listwise)	88						

✔ Double click the table so you can edit it. As was the case with graphs, SPSS has many options to edit statistics in tables as well. Let's try some of them.

✔ Under **Pivot**, select **Transpose Rows and Columns**. Which orientation do you prefer? I like the first since it's more conventional, so I will **Transpose the Rows and Columns** again to return to the original orientation.

✔ Now, click on **Format/Table properties**. Take a moment to view all of the options in this dialog box. "General" allows you to specify the width of cells and the location of labels. "Footnotes" allows you to chose numeric or alphabetic labels and subscript or superscript as the position for those labels. "Cell format" allows you to change the font style and size and the alignment. "Borders" allows you to add or remove borders around rows, columns, and even cells. "Printing" allows you to select options such as rescaling tables to fit on paper. After you've viewed the options, click **Cancel**.

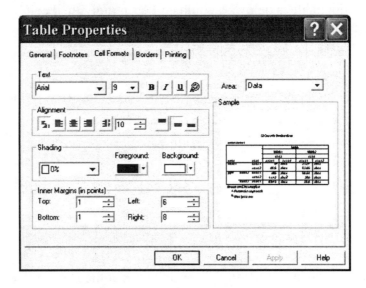

- Now, select **Format/Table Looks**. Scroll through the TableLook Files and look at the samples. If you click **Edit Look** the dialog box from Table Properties will appear and you can alter the appearance of cells, labels, titles, etc to suit your style. Select one you like and click **Ok**. I chose **Academic (narrow)**.

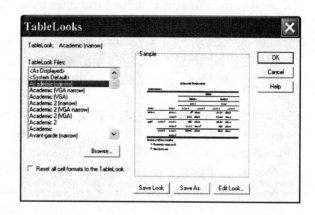

- The resulting table is below. I could edit each individual cell by double clicking on it and then edit the text. For example, I could alter each statistic to include 2 decimal places if I wanted. You try it.

Descriptive Statistics

	N	Range	Minimum	Maximum	Mean	Std. Deviation	Variance
ADD score in elementary school	88	59.0	26.0	85.0	52.602	12.422	154.311
IQ score	88	62.00	75.00	137.00	100.2614	12.9850	168.609
grade in ninth grade English	88	4	0	4	2.66	.95	.894
Grade point average in 9th grade	88	3.33	.67	4.00	2.4562	.8614	.742
Valid N (listwise)	88						

- Now, click on **Window/Data Editor** and look at the standardized values (z scores) SPSS added to your file. A brief portion of the Data Editor appears below. You can see that SPSS named each variable with a z and then truncated the original variable name. SPSS also labeled the new variables. Check this out in Variable View.

dropout	zaddsc	ziq	zengg	zgpa
did not d	-2.1415	Zscore: ADD score in elementary school		
did not d	-1.90001	2.05920	1.41823	1.50186
did not d	-1.81951	.67298	1.41823	1.21165
did not d	-1.57800	.44195	1.41823	1.50186

40

Frequencies

Now, we'll use the frequencies command to help us examine the distributions of the same continuous variables.

✔ Select **Analyze/Descriptive Statistics/Frequency**.

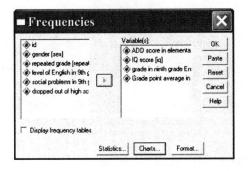

✔ Put the variables of interest in the **Variable** list box. Unselect **Display frequency tables**, because this will be a list of the frequency of every value. Instead, click on **Charts**, select **Histogram with normal curve** and click **Continue**. Now, click **Statistics**.

✔ This dialog box has all of the same options we selected under Descriptives earlier. However, the Descriptives dialog box did not include the median and mode. Select all of the statistics of interest and click **Continue**. Then, click **Ok**. A sample of the output follows.

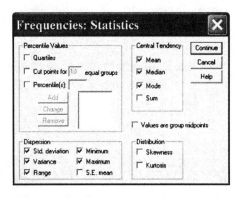

Frequencies

Statistics

		ADD score in elementary school	IQ score	grade in ninth grade English	Grade point average in 9th grade
N	Valid	88	88	88	88
	Missing	0	0	0	0
Mean		52.602	100.2614	2.66	2.4563
Median		50.000	100.0000	3.00	2.6350
Mode		50.0	95.00	3	3.00
Std. Deviation		12.422	12.9850	.95	.8614
Variance		154.311	168.6091	.89	.7421
Range		59.0	62.00	4	3.33
Minimum		26.0	75.00	0	.67
Maximum		85.0	137.00	4	4.00

Histogram

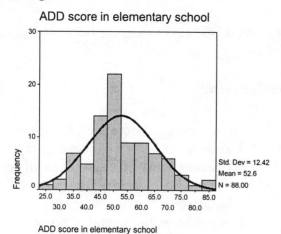

ADD score in elementary school

Take a moment to review the output. It looks like ADD is somewhat normally distributed, though a bit negatively skewed. Looking at your own output, are the other variables normally distributed? I also remember now, that English grade is nominal too. Variables were scored as A, B, C, D, and F. As noted in the text, we could analyze this as continuous data, but it seems that reporting the frequencies rather than measures of central tendency and dispersion may be more appropriate for this variable.

As before, you can edit the tables or the graphs by double clicking on them. One difference we have seen between the Descriptives and Frequencies options is that descriptives only include mean for measures of central tendency whereas Frequencies include the mean, median, and mode. Further, Descriptives does not have any built in graphing options, but Frequencies does.

Now let's use Frequencies to describe categorical data.

✔ Select **Analyze/Descriptive Statistics/Frequencies**.

✔ This time, put gender, level of English class, English grade, repeated a grade, social problems, and drop out status in the variable list. Select **Display frequency table**. Since there is a finite number of values, we want to know how many people fit in every category. Click on **Statistics** and unselect all of the options since we decided measures of central tendency and variability are not useful for these data. Then click **Continue**. Next, click on **Charts**. Click on **Bar chart** and select **Percentages** as the Chart Values. Click **Continue** and then **Ok**. A sample of the resulting output follows. Take a moment to review it.

repeated grade

		Frequency	Percent	Valid Percent	Cumulative Percent
Valid	did not repeate a grade	76	86.4	86.4	86.4
	repeated at least one grade	12	13.6	13.6	100.0
	Total	88	100.0	100.0	

level of English in 9th grade

		Frequency	Percent	Valid Percent	Cumulative Percent
Valid	college prep	14	15.9	15.9	15.9
	general	64	72.7	72.7	88.6
	remedial	10	11.4	11.4	100.0
	Total	88	100.0	100.0	

Gender

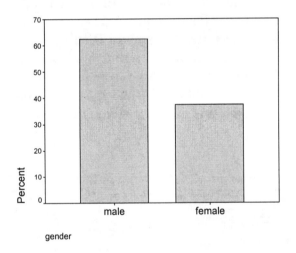

Notice that the frequency tables include a column labeled **Percent** and another labeled **Valid percent**. This is an important distinction when you have missing cases. The percent column indicates the percent of cases in each category out of those cases for which there is complete data on the variable. Valid percent indicates the percent of cases in each category out of the total number of cases, even if some data is missing. For example, imagine a sample of 100 students. Fifty cases are women, 40 are men, and 10 are missing the data. The percent of men would be 44.4%, but the valid percent of men would be 40%. Which do you believe is the more accurate way to describe the sample? I'd argue the valid percent. Now let's move on to a more complicated type of frequency table.

Crosstabs

Sometimes we need to know the number and percent of cases that fall in multiple categories. This is useful when we have multiple categorical variables in a data set. For example, in the data set we have been using, I'd like to know what percent of dropout and nondropouts had social problems. We'll use crosstabs to calculate this.

✔ Click **Analyze/Descriptive Statistics/Crosstabs**.

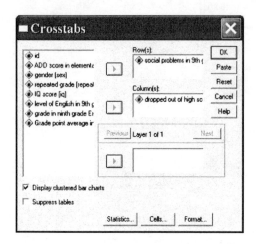

✔ Select social problems for **Rows** and dropped out for **Columns**. Click on **Cells** and select **Observed** for **Counts**, and select **Row**, **Column**, and **Total** under **Percentages**. The click **Continue**. Let's select **Display clustered bar charts** to see if we find this option useful. Then, click **Ok**. The output follows. You can edit both the table and the chart as you have learned.

social problems in 9th grade * dropped out of high school Crosstabulation

			did not drop out	dropped out of high school	Total
social problems in 9th grade	no social problems	Count	73	5	78
		% within social problems in 9th grade	93.6%	6.4%	100.0%
		% within dropped out of high school	93.6%	50.0%	88.6%
		% of Total	83.0%	5.7%	88.6%
	yes, social problems	Count	5	5	10
		% within social problems in 9th grade	50.0%	50.0%	100.0%
		% within dropped out of high school	6.4%	50.0%	11.4%
		% of Total	5.7%	5.7%	11.4%
Total		Count	78	10	88
		% within social problems in 9th grade	88.6%	11.4%	100.0%
		% within dropped out of high school	100.0%	100.0%	100.0%
		% of Total	88.6%	11.4%	100.0%

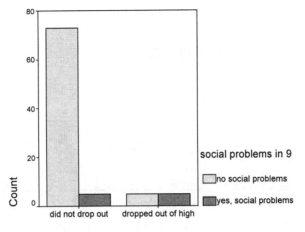

Both the table and the graph show that of those youth with social problems, an equal number did and did not ultimately drop out. This suggests that social problems in ninth grade and drop out status are independent, something we can test later using Chi Square.

Compare Means

Now, let's consider a case where we want to describe a continuous variable but at different levels of a categorical variable. This is often necessary when you are comparing group means. For example, we can compare ADD symptoms for males and females. Let's try it together.

✔ Select **Analyze/Compare Means/Means**. Notice this is the first time we haven't selected Descriptive Statistics in this chapter.

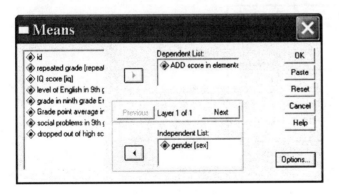

✔ Select ADD score for the **Dependent List** and Gender for the **Independent List**. Click **Options**. Notice that mean, standard deviation and number of cases are already selected under statistics. Add any other descriptive you are interested in, then click **Continue** and then **Ok**. The output follows.

Report

ADD score in elementary school

gender	Mean	N	Std. Deviation
male	54.291	55	12.902
female	49.788	33	11.205
Total	52.602	88	12.422

Do you think males and females differed in their ADD symptoms?

Let's try another more complicated example. This time, let's calculate descriptives for ADD symptoms broken down by gender and whether or not a child had social problems.

✔ Select **Analyze/Compare Means/Means**.

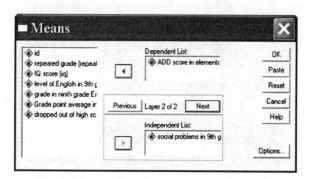

✔ Just like before, select ADD score for the **Dependent List**, and gender for the **Layer 1 Independent List**. Then click **Next**. Select social problems as the **Layer 2 Independent List**. Select whatever statistics you want under **Options** and then click **Continue** and **Ok**. The output is below.

Report

ADD score in elementary school

gender	social problems in	Mean	N	Std. Deviation
male	no social problems	52.250	48	11.613
	yes, social problems	68.286	7	13.413
	Total	54.291	55	12.902
female	no social problems	48.900	30	11.183
	yes, social problems	58.667	3	8.083
	Total	49.788	33	11.205
Total	no social problems	50.962	78	11.494
	yes, social problems	65.400	10	12.492
	Total	52.602	88	12.422

Notice that this table gives you the marginal descriptives (i.e., the descriptive for gender independent of social problems and vice versa) under totals and the cell descriptives (i.e., the descriptives at each level of the variables-e.g., for boys with social problems).

✓ **Exit** SPSS. There is no need to save the Data File since we haven't changed it. It is up to you to decide whether or not you would like to save the output file for future reference.

We've reviewed a variety of options for calculating descriptive statistics depending on the type of data and the kinds of questions. We've also seen that many of the graphs we reviewed in Chapter 3 are options in the subcommands under Descriptive Statistics. In the following chapters you will discover that descriptive statistics are an option embedded within many other analyses dialog boxes (e.g. t-test, ANOVA, etc). Try the following exercises to be sure you understand all of the various options for calculating descriptives and to help you identify your own preferences.

Exercises

1. Using *merge1.sav,* calculate the mean, median, mode, range, variance, and standard deviation for the following variables: self-esteem, anxiety, coping, and health. Create a histogram for anxiety. Note how you did each.

2. Using the data in *Appenidx D.sav*, calculate the frequency and percent of females and males who did and did not have social problems.

3. Using the data in *Appenidx D.sav*, calculate the mean, variance, and standard deviation for GPA broken down by social problems and drop out status.

5. Correlation

Objectives

- ◆ Calculate correlations
- ◆ Calculate correlations for subgroups using split file
- ◆ Create scatterplots with lines of best fit for subgroups and multiple correlations

Correlation

The first inferential statistic we will focus on is correlation. As noted in the text, correlation is used to test the degree of association between variables. All of the inferential statistics commands in SPSS are accessed from the Analyze menu. Let's open SPSS and replicate the correlation between height and weight presented in the textbook in Figure 9.8

✓ **Open** *height and weight.sav*. Take a moment to review the data file.

✓ Under **Analyze**, select **Correlate/Bivariate**. Bivariate means we are examining the simple association between 2 variables.

✓ In the dialog box, select height and weight for **Variables**. Select **Pearson** for **Correlation Coefficients** since the data are continuous. The default for **Tests of Significance** is **Two-tailed**. You could change it to One-tailed if you have a directional hypothesis. Selecting **Flag significant correlations** means that the significant correlations will be noted in the output by asterisks. This is a nice feature. Then click **Options**.

- Now you can see how descriptive statistics are built into other menus. Select **Means and standard deviations** under **Statistics**. Missing Values are important. In large data sets, pieces of data are often missing for some

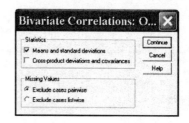

variables. For example I may run correlations between height, weight, and blood pressure. One subject may be missing blood pressure data. If I check **Exclude cases listwise**, SPSS will not include that person's data in the correlation between height and weight, even though those data are not missing. If I check **Exclude cases pairwise,** SPSS will include that person's data to calculate any correlations that do not involved blood pressure. In this case, the person's data would still be reflected in the correlation between height and weight. You have to decide whether or not you want to exclude cases that are missing any data from all analyses. (Normally it is much safer to go with listwise deletion, even though it will reduce your sample size.) In this case, it doesn't matter because there is no missing data. Click **Continue**. When you return to the previous dialog box, click **Ok**. The output follow.

Correlations

Descriptive Statistics

	Mean	Std. Deviation	N
HEIGHT	68.72	3.66	92
WEIGHT	145.15	23.74	92

Correlations

		HEIGHT	WEIGHT
HEIGHT	Pearson Correlation	1.000	.785**
	Sig. (2-tailed)	.	.000
	N	92	92
WEIGHT	Pearson Correlation	.785**	1.000
	Sig. (2-tailed)	.000	.
	N	92	92

**. Correlation is significant at the 0.01 level

Notice, the correlation coefficient is .785 and is statistically significant, just as reported in the textbook. In the textbook, Howell made the point that heterogeneous samples effect correlation coefficients. In this example, we included both males and females. Let's examine the correlation separately for males and females as was done in the text.

Subgroup Correlations

We need to get SPSS to calculate the correlation between height and weight separately for males and females. The easiest way to do this is to split our data file by sex. Let's try this together.

✔ In the Data Editor window, select **Data/Split** file.

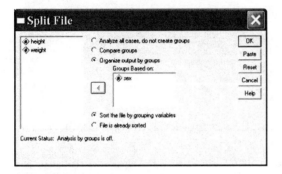

✔ Select **Organize output by groups** and **Groups Based on** sex. This means that any analyses you specify will be run separately for males and females. Then, click **Ok**.

✔ Notice that the order of the data file has been changed. It is now sorted by sex, with males at the top of the file.

✔ Now, select **Analyze/Correlation/Bivariate**. The same variables and options you selected last time are still in the dialog box. Take a moment to check to see for yourself. Then, click **Ok**. The output follow broken down by males and females.

Correlations

SEX = Male

Descriptive Statistics[a]

	Mean	Std. Deviation	N
HEIGHT	70.75	2.58	57
WEIGHT	158.26	18.64	57

a. SEX = Male

Correlations[a]

		HEIGHT	WEIGHT
HEIGHT	Pearson Correlation	1.000	.604**
	Sig. (2-tailed)	.	.000
	N	57	57
WEIGHT	Pearson Correlation	.604**	1.000
	Sig. (2-tailed)	.000	.
	N	57	57

**. Correlation is significant at the 0.01 level

a. SEX = Male

SEX = Female

Descriptive Statistics[a]

	Mean	Std. Deviation	N
HEIGHT	65.40	2.56	35
WEIGHT	123.80	13.37	35

a. SEX = Female

Correlations[a]

		HEIGHT	WEIGHT
HEIGHT	Pearson Correlation	1.000	.494**
	Sig. (2-tailed)	.	.003
	N	35	35
WEIGHT	Pearson Correlation	.494**	1.000
	Sig. (2-tailed)	.003	.
	N	35	35

**. Correlation is significant at the 0.01 level

a. SEX = Female

As before, our results replicate those in the textbook. The correlation between height and weight is stronger for males than females. Now let's see if we can create a more complicated scatterplot that illustrates the pattern of correlation for males and females on one graph. First, we need to turn off split file.

✔ Select **Data/Split file** from the Data Editor window. Then select **Analyze all cases, do not compare groups** and click **Ok**. Now, we can proceed.

Scatterplots of Data by Subgroups

✔ Select **Graphs/Scatter**. Then, select **Simple** and click **Define**.

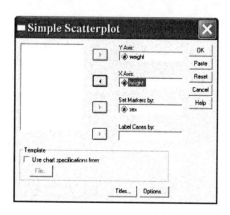

✔ To be consistent with the graph in the text book, select weight as the **Y Axis** and height as the **X Axis**. Then, select sex for **Set Markers by**. This means SPSS will distinguish the males dots from the female dots on the graph. Then, click **Ok**.

When your graph appears, you will see that the only way males and females are distinct from one another is by color. This distinction may not show up well, so let's edit the graph.

✔ Double click the graph to activate the Chart Editor. Then click on the female dots on the plot. SPSS will highlight them. The click the Marker icon.

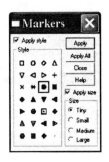

✔ Select the solid circle under **Style** and click **Apply**. Then click on the male dots, and select the open circle in **Style** and click **Apply**. Then, close the dialog box. The resulting graph should look just like the one in the textbook. I'd like to alter our graph to include the line of best fit for both groups.

✔ Click on **Chart/Options**.

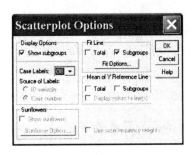

✔ Under **Fit Line** select **Subgroups**. Then click **Fit Options**. Select **Linear Regression** and click **Continue**. Then, click **Ok**. The resulting graph follows.

✔ Edit the graph to suit your style as you learned in Chapter 3 (e.g., add a title, change the axes titles and legend).

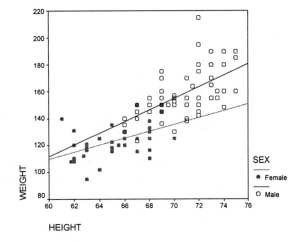

This more complex scatterplot nicely illustrates the difference in the correlation between height and weight for males and females. Let's move on to a more complicated example.

Overlay Scatterplots

Another kind of scatterplot that might be useful is one that displays the association between different independent variables with the same dependant variable. Above, we compared the same correlation for different groups. This time, we want to compare different correlations. Let's use the course evaluation example from the textbook that is discussed in Figure 9.10 It looks like expected grade is more strongly related to ratings of fairness of the exam than ratings of instructor knowledge. I'd like to plot both correlations. I can reasonably plot them on the same graph since all of the questions were rated on the same scale.

✔ **Open** *course evaluations.sav*. You do not need to save *height and weight.sav* since you did not change it. So click **No**.

✔ First, let's make sure the correlations reported in the text in Figure 9.10 are accurate. Click **Analyze/Correlation/Bivariate** and select all of the variables. Click **Ok**. The output follow. Do they agree with the textbook?

Correlations

		OVERALL	TEACH	EXAM	KNOWLEDG	GRADE	ENROLL
OVERALL	Pearson Correlation	1.000	.804**	.596**	.682**	.301*	-.240
	Sig. (2-tailed)	.	.000	.000	.000	.034	.094
	N	50	50	50	50	50	50
TEACH	Pearson Correlation	.804**	1.000	.720**	.526**	.469**	-.451**
	Sig. (2-tailed)	.000	.	.000	.000	.001	.001
	N	50	50	50	50	50	50
EXAM	Pearson Correlation	.596**	.720**	1.000	.451**	.610**	-.558**
	Sig. (2-tailed)	.000	.000	.	.001	.000	.000
	N	50	50	50	50	50	50
KNOWLEDG	Pearson Correlation	.682**	.526**	.451**	1.000	.224	-.128
	Sig. (2-tailed)	.000	.000	.001	.	.118	.376
	N	50	50	50	50	50	50
GRADE	Pearson Correlation	.301*	.469**	.610**	.224	1.000	-.337*
	Sig. (2-tailed)	.034	.001	.000	.118	.	.017
	N	50	50	50	50	50	50
ENROLL	Pearson Correlation	-.240	-.451**	-.558**	-.128	-.337*	1.000
	Sig. (2-tailed)	.094	.001	.000	.376	.017	.
	N	50	50	50	50	50	50

**. Correlation is significant at the 0.01 level (2-tailed).

*. Correlation is significant at the 0.05 level (2-tailed).

Now, let's make our scatterplot.

✔ Select **Graphs/Scatter**. Then select **Overlay** and click **Define**.

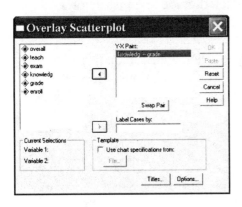

✔ Click on knowledge and grade and shift them into **Y-X Pairs**. Then click on exam and knowledge and click them into **Y-X pairs**. Since grade is the commonality between both pairs, I'd like it to be on the Y axis. To make this change, highlight each pair one at a time and click **Swap Pair**. Grade should then appear first for both. Then, click **Ok**.

✔ As in the previous example, the dots are distinguished by color. Double click the graph and use the **Marker** icon to make them more distinct as you learned above.

✔ Click **Chart/Options**.

✔ Select **Display for each pair** under **Fit Line**. Then click **Fit Options**, select **Linear Regression**, and click **Continue**. Then, click **Ok**. My final graph appears below.

Note that the axes are not labeled. You could label the Y Axis Grade. But you could not label the X axis because it represents two different variables-- exam and knowledge. That is why the legend is necessary.

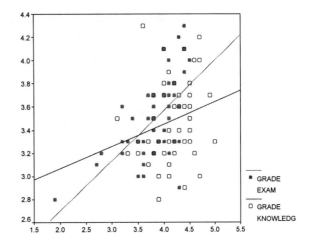

As you can see, the association between expected grade and fairness of the exam is stronger than the correlation between expected grade and instructor's knowledge.

Now, you should have the tools necessary to calculate Pearson Correlations and to create various scatterplots that compliment those correlations. Complete the following exercises to help you internalize these steps.

Exercises

Exercises 1 through 3 are based on *Appenidx D.sav*.

1. Calculate the correlations between Add symptoms, IQ, GPA, and English grade twice, once using a one-tailed test and once using a two-tailed test. Does this make a difference? Typically, when would this make a difference.

2. Calculate the same correlations separately for those who did and did not drop out, using a two-tailed test. Are they similar or different?

3. Create a scatterplot illustrating the correlation between IQ score and GPA for those who did and did not drop out. Be sure to include the line of best fit for each group.

4. Open *course evaluation.sav*. Create a scatterplot for fairness of exams and teacher skills and fairness of exam and instructor knowledge on one graph. Be sure to include the lines of best fit. Describe your graph.

6: Regression and Multiple Regression

Objectives

♦ Calculate regressions with one independent variable
♦ Calculate regressions with multiple independent variables
♦ Scatterplot of predicted and actual values
♦ Calculating residuals and predicted values

Regression

Regression allows you to predict variables based on another variable. In this chapter we will focus on linear regression or relationships that are linear (a line) rather than curvilinear (a curve) in nature. Let's begin with the example used in the textbook illustrated in Table 10.2 in which mental health symptoms are predicted from stress.

✔ **Open** *symptoms and stress.sav.*

✔ Select **Analyze/Regression/Linear**.

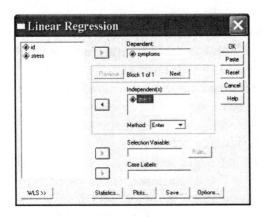

✔ Select symptoms as the **Dependent** variable and stress as the **Independent** variable. Then, click on **Statistics** to explore our options. The following dialog box will appear.

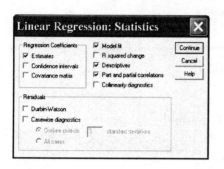

✔ As you can see there are many options. We will focus only on information covered in the textbook. **Estimates** and **Model Fit** are selected by default. Leave them that way. Then select **Descriptives** and **Part and partial correlations**. SPSS will then calculate the mean and standard deviation for each variable in the equation and the correlation between the two variables. Then, click **Continue**.

✔ At the main dialog box, click on **Plots** so we can see our options.

✔ It looks like we can create scatterplots here. Click **Help** to see what the abbreviations represent. I'd like to plot the Dependent variable against the predicted values to see how close they are. Select **Dependnt** for **Y** and **Adjpred** for **X**. Adjpred is the adjusted prediction. Used **Help/Topics/Index** to find out what this means for yourself. Then, click **Continue**.

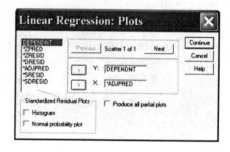

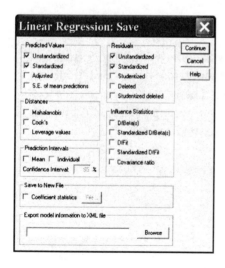

✔ In the main dialog box, click **Save**, and the dialog box to the left will appear. For **Predicted Values**, select **Unstandardized** and **Standardized**. For **Residuals**, also select **Unstandardized** and **Standardized**. Now, SPSS will save the predicted values of symptoms based on the regression equation and the residual or difference between the predicted values and actual values of symptoms in the data file. This is a nice feature. Remember, the standardized values are based on z score transformations of the data whereas the unstandardized values are based on the raw data. Click **Continue**.

✔ Finally, click on **Options**.

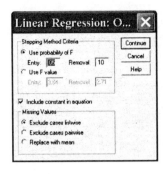

✔ Including a constant in the equation is selected by default. That's good. We will always leave this checked. Excluding cases listwise is also fine. We do not have any missing cases in this example anyway. Click **Continue**, and then **Ok** in the main dialog box. The output follows.

Regression

Descriptive Statistics

	Mean	Std. Deviation	N
SYMPTOMS	90.70	20.27	107
STRESS	21.47	13.10	107

Correlations

		SYMPTOMS	STRESS
Pearson Correlation	SYMPTOMS	1.000	.506
	STRESS	.506	1.000
Sig. (1-tailed)	SYMPTOMS	.	.000
	STRESS	.000	.
N	SYMPTOMS	107	107
	STRESS	107	107

Variables Entered/Removed[b]

Model	Variables Entered	Variables Removed	Method
1	STRESS[a]	.	Enter

a. All requested variables entered.

b. Dependent Variable: SYMPTOMS

Model Summary[b]

Model	R	R Square	Adjusted R Square	Std. Error of the Estimate
1	.506[a]	.256	.249	17.56

a. Predictors: (Constant), STRESS

b. Dependent Variable: SYMPTOMS

ANOVA[b]

Model		Sum of Squares	df	Mean Square	F	Sig.
1	Regression	11148.382	1	11148.382	36.145	.000[a]
	Residual	32386.048	105	308.439		
	Total	43534.430	106			

a. Predictors: (Constant), STRESS

b. Dependent Variable: SYMPTOMS

Coefficients[a]

Model		Unstandardized Coefficients		Standardized Coefficients	t	Sig.	Correlations		
		B	Std. Error	Beta			Zero-order	Partial	Part
1	(Constant)	73.890	3.271		22.587	.000			
	STRESS	.783	.130	.506	6.012	.000	.506	.506	.506

a. Dependent Variable: SYMPTOMS

Charts

Scatterplot

Dependent Variable: SYMPTOMS

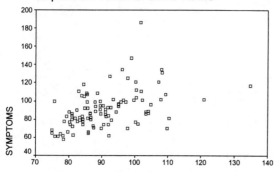

Regression Adjusted (Press) Predicted Value

✔ How does our output compare to the output presented in the textbook in Figure 10.3? Take a moment to identify all of the key pieces of information. Find r^2, find the ANOVA used to test the significance of the model, find the regression coefficients used to calculate the regression equation. One difference is that the textbook did not include the scatterplot. What do you think of the scatterplot? Does it help you see that predicting symptoms based on stress is a pretty good estimate? You could add a line of best fit to the scatterplot using what you learned in Chapter 5.

✔ Now, click **Window/Data Editor** and look at the new data (residuals and predicted values) in your file. A small sample is below. Note how they are named and labeled.

	id	stress	symptoms	pre_1	res_1	zpr_1	zre_1
1	1	30	99	97.3830	Unstandardized Predicted Value		09207
2	2	27	94	95.03368	-1.03368	.42248	-.05886
3	3	9	80	80.93762	-.93762	-.95202	-.05339
4	4	20	70	89.55188	-19.5519	-.11204	-1.11328

Let's use what we know about the regression equation to check the accuracy of the scores created by SPSS. We will focus on the unstandardized predicted and residual values. This is also a great opportunity to learn how to use the Transform menus to perform calculations based on existing data.

We know from the regression equation that:

Symptoms Predicted or $\hat{Y} = 73.890 + .783*$ Stress.

We also know that the residual can be computed as follows:

Residual = Y- $\hat{Y}$ or Symptoms – Symptoms Predicted Values.

We'll use SPSS to calculate these values and then compare them to the values computed by SPSS.

✔ In the Data Editor window, select **Transform/Compute**.

✔ Under **Target Variable**, type sympred. This will be the name of the new variable, symptoms predicted, we are calculating. Click on **Type & Label** to specify a variable label. Click **Continue** when done. Then, we need to type the regression equation where it says **Numeric Expression**. Simply type 73.890 + .783* or use your mouse to click on the numbers and characters in the dialog box. Then highlight stress and either click the arrow or double click on stress to move stress into the equation. Then, click **OK**.

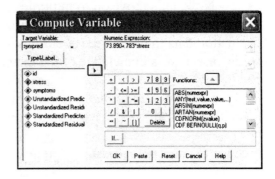

- ✔ Check the Data Editor to see if your new variable is there, and compare it to pre_1. Are they the same? The only difference I see is that our variable is only expressed to 2 decimal places. But, the values agree.

- ✔ Follow similar steps to calculate the residual. Click on **Transform/Compute**. Name your **Target Variable** sympres and **Label** it symptoms residual. Put the formula symptoms-sympred in the **Numeric Expression** box by double clicking the two pre-existing variables and typing a minus sign between them. Then, click **Ok**.

- ✔ Compare these values to res_1. Again they agree. A portion of the new data file is below.

	id	stress	symptoms	pre_1	res_1	zpr_1	zre_1	sympred	sympres
1	1	30	99	97.38302	1.61698	.65157	.09207		Symptoms Predicted
2	2	27	94	95.03368	-1.03368	.42248	-.05886	95.03	-1.03
3	3	9	80	80.93762	-.93762	-.95202	-.05339	80.94	-.94
4	4	20	70	89.55188	-19.5519	-.11204	-1.11328	89.55	-19.55

Now that you are confident that the predicted and residual values computed by SPSS are exactly what you intended, you won't ever need to calculate them yourself again. You can simply rely on the values computed by SPSS through the Save command.

Multiple Regression

Now, let's move on to multiple regression. We will predict the dependent variable from multiple independent variables. This time we will use the course evaluation data to predict the overall rating of lectures based on ratings of teaching skills, instructor's knowledge of the material, and expected grade.

- ✔ **Open** course evaluations.sav. You may want to save symptoms and stress.sav to include the residuals. That's up to you.

- ✔ Select **Analyze/Regression/Linear**.

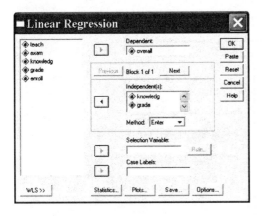

✓ Select overall as the **Dependent** variable, and teach, knowledge, and grade as the **Independents**. Since there are multiple independent variables, we need to think about the Method of entry. As noted in the text, stepwise procedures are seductive, but we want to select **Enter** meaning all of the predictors will be entered simultaneously.

✓ Click **Statistics** and select **Descriptives** and **Part and partial correlations**. Click **Continue**.

✓ Click **Plots** and select **Dependnt** as **Y** and **Adjpred** as **X**. Click **Continue**.

✓ Click **Save** and select the **Residuals** and **Predicted** values of your choice. Click **Continue**.

✓ Click **Ok** at the main dialog box. The output follows.

Regression

Descriptive Statistics

	Mean	Std. Deviation	N
OVERALL	3.55	.61	50
TEACH	3.66	.53	50
KNOWLEDG	4.18	.41	50
GRADE	3.49	.35	50

Correlations

		OVERALL	TEACH	KNOWLEDG	GRADE
Pearson Correlation	OVERALL	1.000	.804	.682	.301
	TEACH	.804	1.000	.526	.469
	KNOWLEDG	.682	.526	1.000	.224
	GRADE	.301	.469	.224	1.000
Sig. (1-tailed)	OVERALL	.	.000	.000	.017
	TEACH	.000	.	.000	.000
	KNOWLEDG	.000	.000	.	.059
	GRADE	.017	.000	.059	.
N	OVERALL	50	50	50	50
	TEACH	50	50	50	50
	KNOWLEDG	50	50	50	50
	GRADE	50	50	50	50

Variables Entered/Removed[b]

Model	Variables Entered	Variables Removed	Method
1	GRADE, KNOWLEDG, TEACH[a]		Enter

a. All requested variables entered.

b. Dependent Variable: OVERALL

Model Summary[b]

Model	R	R Square	Adjusted R Square	Std. Error of the Estimate
1	.863[a]	.745	.728	.32

a. Predictors: (Constant), GRADE, KNOWLEDG, TEACH

b. Dependent Variable: OVERALL

ANOVA[b]

Model		Sum of Squares	df	Mean Square	F	Sig.
1	Regression	13.737	3	4.579	44.741	.000[a]
	Residual	4.708	46	.102		
	Total	18.445	49			

a. Predictors: (Constant), GRADE, KNOWLEDG, TEACH

b. Dependent Variable: OVERALL

Coefficients^a

Model		Unstandardized Coefficients		Standardized Coefficients	t	Sig.
		B	Std. Error	Beta		
1	(Constant)	-.927	.596		-1.556	.127
	TEACH	.759	.112	.658	6.804	.000
	KNOWLEDG	.534	.132	.355	4.052	.000
	GRADE	-.153	.147	-.088	-1.037	.305

a. Dependent Variable: OVERALL

Charts

Scatterplot

Dependent Variable: OVERALL

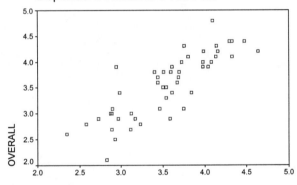

Regression Adjusted (Press) Predicted Value

✔ Compare this output to the results in the textbook in Table 11.3. Notice the values are the same, but the styles are different since the output in the book is from Minitab, a different data analysis program.

✔ **Exit** SPSS. It's up to you to decide if you want to save the changes to the data file and the output file.

In this chapter, you have learned to use SPSS to calculate simple and multiple regressions. You have also learned how to use built in menus to calculate descriptives, residuals and predicted values, and to create various scatterplots. As you can see, SPSS has really simplified the process. Complete the following exercises to increase your comfort and familiarity with all of the options.

Exercises

1. Using data in *course evaluations.sav*, predict overall quality from expected grade.

2. To increase your comfort with Transform, calculate the predicted overall score based on the regression equation from the previous exercise. Then calculate the residual. Did you encounter any problems?

3. Using data in *height and weight.sav*, predict weight from height and gender. Compare your results to the output in Table 11.6 of the textbook.

4. Using the data in *cancer patients.sav*, predict distress at time 2 from distress at time 1, blame person, and blame behavior. Compare your output to the results presented in Table 11.7 in the textbook.

7. Comparing Means Using t-tests.

Objectives

  ♦ Calculate one sample t-tests
  ♦ Calculate paired samples t-tests
  ♦ Calculate independent samples t-tests
  ♦ Graphically represent mean differences

In this chapter, we will learn to compare means using t-tests. We will cover information that is presented in the textbook in Chapters, 12, 13, and 14. One important thing to note is that SPSS uses the term paired sample t-test to reflect what the textbook refers to as related samples t-tests. They are the same thing.

One Sample t-tests

One sample t-tests are typically used to compare a sample mean to a known population mean. Let's use the moon illusion example illustrated in Section 12.5 of the textbook. We want to know if there was a moon illusion using the apparatus. If there was, the obtained ratio should not equal 1. Let's try this together.

✔ **Open** *moon illusion.sav*.

✔ Select **Analyze/Compare Means/One-Sample t-test**.

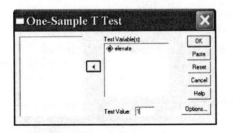

✔ Select elevate as the **Test Variable**. Type 1 in as the **Test Value**. We are testing the null hypothesis that the sample mean = 1. Then, click **Options**.

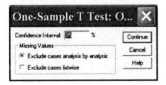

✔ Notice, SPSS allows us to specify what **Confidence Interval** to calculate. Leave it at 95%. Click **Continue** and then **Ok**. The output follows.

T-Test

One-Sample Statistics

	N	Mean	Std. Deviation	Std. Error Mean
ELEVATE	10	1.46	.34	.11

One-Sample Test

	Test Value = 1					
					95% Confidence Interval of the Difference	
	t	df	Sig. (2-tailed)	Mean Difference	Lower	Upper
ELEVATE	4.298	9	.002	.46	.22	.71

✔ Notice that descriptive statistics are automatically calculated in the one-sample t-test. Does our t-value agree with the one in the textbook? Look at the **Confidence Interval.** Notice that it is not the confidence interval of the mean, but the confidence interval for the difference between the sample mean and the test value we specified, in this case 1.

Now, let's move on to related or paired samples t-tests.

Paired Samples t-tests

A paired samples t-test is used to compare two related means. It tests the null hypothesis that the difference between two related means is 0. Let's begin with the example in Table 13.1 in the textbook. We want to see if the difference in weight before and after a family therapy intervention is significantly different from 0.

✔ **Open** *anorexia family therapy.sav*. You don't need to save *moon illusion.sav* since we didn't change the data file.

✔ Select **Analyze/Compare Means/Paired Samples t-test**.

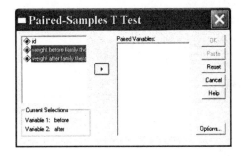

✔ Select weight before and weight after family therapy and click them into the **Paired Variables** box using the arrow. Then click **Options**. Notice you can select the confidence interval you want again. Leave it at 95%, click **Continue**, and then click **Ok**. The output follows.

T-Test

Paired Samples Statistics

		Mean	N	Std. Deviation	Std. Error Mean
Pair 1	weight before family therapy	83.2294	17	5.0167	1.2167
	weight after family therapy	90.4941	17	8.4751	2.0555

Paired Samples Correlations

		N	Correlation	Sig.
Pair 1	weight before family therapy & weight after family therapy	17	.538	.026

Paired Samples Test

| | | Paired Differences | | | | | | | |
| | | | | | 95% Confidence Interval of the Difference | | | | |
		Mean	Std. Deviation	Std. Error Mean	Lower	Upper	t	df	Sig. (2-tailed)
Pair 1	weight before family therapy - weight after family therapy	-7.2647	7.1574	1.7359	-10.9447	-3.5847	-4.185	16	.001

✔ Notice, the descriptives were automatically calculated again. Compare this output to the results in the textbook. Are they in agreement? The mean difference is negative here because weight after the treatment was subtracted from weight before the treatment. So the mean difference really shows that subjects tended to weigh more after the treatment. If you get confused by the sign of the difference, just look at the mean values for the before and after weights. Notice that this time the confidence interval is consistent with what we would expect. It suggests we can be 95% confident that the actual weight gain of the population of anorexics receiving family therapy is within the calculated limits.

✔ If you want to see the mean difference graphically, try to make a bar graph using what you learned in Chapter 3. [Hint: Select **Graphs/Bar**, then select **Simple** and **Summaries of separate variables**. Select weight before and weight after family therapy for **Bars Represent**. Use mean as the **Summary** score. Click **Ok**. Edit your graph to suit your style.] Mine appears below.

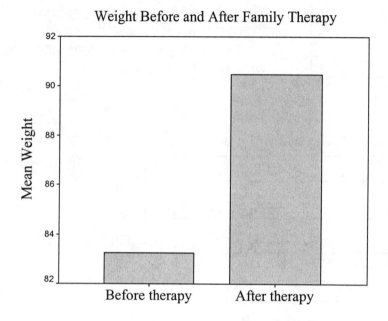

Weight Before and After Family Therapy

Independent Samples t-test

An independent samples t-test is used to compare means from independent groups. Let's try one together using the horn honking example in the textbook in Figures 14.3 and 14.4. We will test the hypothesis that people will honk more quickly to low status cars than to high status cars.

✔ **Open** *horn honking.sav*. You don't need to save *anorexia family therapy.sav* since we did not change the data file.

✔ Select **Analyze/Compare Means/Independent Samples t-test**.

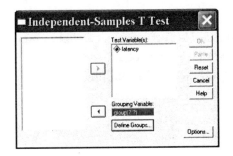

✔ Select latency as the **Test Variable** and group as the **Grouping Variable**. Then, click **Define Groups**.

✔ Type 1 for **Group 1** and 2 for **Group 2,** to indicate what groups are being compared. Then, click **Continue**. The **Options** are the same as the other kinds of t-tests. Look at them if you would like. Then, click **Ok**. The output follows.

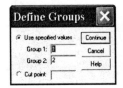

T-Test

Group Statistics

	GROUP	N	Mean	Std. Deviation	Std. Error Mean
LATENCY	Low status	15	7.1200	2.7727	.7159
	High status	20	9.2305	2.8203	.6306

Independent Samples Test

		Levene's Test for Equality of Variances		t-test for Equality of Means						
									95% Confidence Interval of the Difference	
		F	Sig.	t	df	Sig. (2-tailed)	Mean Difference	Std. Error Difference	Lower	Upper
LATENCY	Equal variances assumed	.024	.877	-2.207	33	.034	-2.1105	.9564	-4.0564	-.1646
	Equal variances not assumed			-2.212	30.586	.035	-2.1105	.9541	-4.0574	-.1636

✔ As before, the descriptives were calculated automatically. Remember, with an independent groups t-test, we are concerned with homogeneity of variance because it determines whether or not to use the pooled variance when calculating t. Since **Levene's test for the equality of variances** is not significant, we know the variances are not significantly different, so they can be pooled. Thus, we will use the t reported in the row labeled **Equal variances assumed**. Compare this value to the t value reported in Figure 14.3 in the textbook. The results support the hypotheses that people honk more quickly in response to low status than high status cars.

Now, let's create a bar graph to illustrate this group difference.

- Select **Graphs/Bar**. Then select **Simple** and **Summaries for groups of cases** and click **Define**. Then select latency for **Bars Represent**, and select group for **Category Axis**. Click **Ok**. Edit the graph to suit your style. My graph follows.

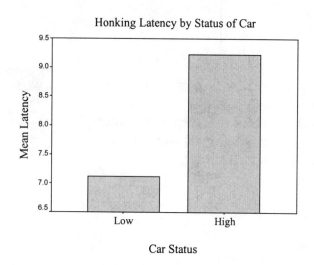

In this chapter, you have learned to calculate each of the 3 types of t-tests covered in the textbook. You have learned to display mean differences graphically as well. Complete the following exercises to help you internalize when each type of t-test should be used.

Exercises

1. Use the data in *sat.sav* to compare the scores of students who did not see the reading passage to the score you would expect if they were just guessing (20) using a one-sample t test. Compare your results to the results in the textbook in Section 12.9. What conclusions can you draw from this example?

2. Open *moon illusion paired.sav*. Use a paired samples t-test to examine the difference in the moon illusion in the eyes elevated and the eyes level conditions. Compare your results to the results presented in Section 13.3 in the textbook.

3. Create a bar graph to display the difference, or lack thereof, in the moon illusion in the eyes level and eye elevated conditions, from the previous exercise.

4. Using the data in *horn honking.sav*, create a boxplot illustrating the group differences in latencies for low status and high status cars. Compare your boxplot to the one in the textbook in Figure 14.3.

5. Open *anorexia weight gain.sav*. In this data set, weight gain was calculated for three groups of anorexics. One group received family therapy, another cognitive behavioral therapy, and the final group was a control group. Use an independent samples t-test to compare weight gain between the control group and family therapy group. Compare your results to the data presented in the textbook in Table 14.1.

6. In the same data set, use independent t-tests to compare the weight gain for the cognitive behavior therapy and control group and for the two therapy groups. Now that you have compared each of the groups, what conclusions would you draw about which type of therapy is most effective?

7. Using the same data set, create a bar graph or box plot that illustrates weight gain for all 3 groups.

8. Comparing Means Using One Way ANOVA

Objectives

- ◆ Calculate a one-way analysis of variance
- ◆ Run various multiple comparisons
- ◆ Calculate measures of effect size

A One Way ANOVA is an analysis of variance in which there is only one independent variable. It can be used to compare mean differences in 2 or more groups. In SPSS, you can calculate one-way ANOVAS in two different ways. One way is through Analyze/Compare Means/One-Way ANOVA and the other is through Analyze/General Linear Model/Univariate. We'll try both in this chapter so we can compare them.

One-Way ANOVA

Let's begin with an example in the textbook illustrated in Table 16.5. Maternal role adaptation was compared in a group of mothers of low birth-weight (LBW) infants who had been in an experimental intervention, mothers of LBW infants who were in a control group, and mothers of full-term infants. The hypothesis was that mothers of LBW infants in the experimental intervention would adapt to their maternal role as well as mothers of healthy full-term infants, and each of these groups would adapt better than mothers of LBW infants in the control group.

✔ **Open** *maternal role adaptation.sav.*

✔ Select **Analyze/Compare Means/One-Way ANOVA**.

✔ Select maternal role adaptation for the
Dependent List since it is the dependent
variable. Select group as the **Factor** or
independent variable. Then click **Post Hoc** to
see various options for calculating multiple
comparisons. If the ANOVA is significant,
we can use the post hoc tests to determine
which specific groups differ significantly
from one another.

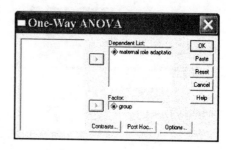

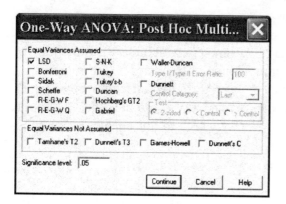

✔ As you can see, there are
many options. Let's select
LSD under **Equal Variances
Assumed** since it is Fisher's
Least Significant Difference
Test which is calculated in the
text, except that SPSS will test
the differences even if the
overall F is not significant.

✔ Note that .05 is the default under **Significance level**. After consulting with SPSS
technical support, it is clear that this is the experiment-wise or family-wise
significance level. So any comparison flagged by SPSS as significant is based on
a Bonferroni Type Correction. You do not need to adjust the significance level
yourself.

✔ Click **Options**. In the next dialog box, select
Descriptives under **Statistics**, and select **Means plot** so
SPSS will create a graph of the group means for us. The
default under **Missing Values** is **Exclude cases analysis
by analysis**. Let's leave this as is. Click **Continue** and
then **Ok**. The output follows.

Oneway

Descriptives

maternal role adaptation (low sores better)

	N	Mean	Std. Deviation	Std. Error	95% Confidence Interval for Mean		Minimum	Maximum
					Lower Bound	Upper Bound		
LBW Experimental	29	14.96552	4.84387	.89948	13.12301	16.80803	10.00	29.00
LBW Control	27	18.33333	5.16646	.99429	16.28955	20.37712	10.00	29.00
Full-term	37	14.83784	3.70820	.60962	13.60146	16.07421	10.00	25.00
Total	93	15.89247	4.74677	.49222	14.91489	16.87006	10.00	29.00

ANOVA

maternal role adaptation (low s ores better)

	Sum of Squares	df	Mean Square	F	Sig.
Between Groups	226.932	2	113.466	5.532	.005
Within Groups	1845.993	90	20.511		
Total	2072.925	92			

Post Hoc Tests

Multiple Comparisons

Dependent Variable: maternal role adaptation (low sores better)

LSD

(I) GROUP	(J) GROUP	Mean Difference (I-J)	Std. Error	Sig.	95% Confidence Interval	
					Lower Bound	Upper Bound
LBW Experimental	LBW Control	-3.36782*	1.21117	.007	-5.77403	-.96161
	Full-term	.12768	1.12322	.910	-2.10380	2.35916
LBW Control	LBW Experimental	3.36782*	1.21117	.007	.96161	5.77403
	Full-term	3.49550*	1.14631	.003	1.21816	5.77283
Full-term	LBW Experimental	-.12768	1.12322	.910	-2.35916	2.10380
	LBW Control	-3.49550*	1.14631	.003	-5.77283	-1.21816

*. The mean difference is significant at the .05 level.

Means Plots

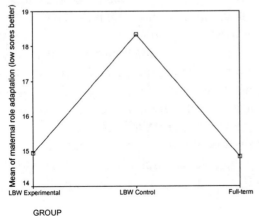

GROUP

77

✔ Compare this output to the results presented in Table 16.5 and 16.7 of the textbook.

We can see the descriptive statistics and the F value are the same. It is harder to compare the post hoc comparisons because SPSS does not display the t values. They simply report the mean difference and the significance level. The important thing to note is that the conclusions we can draw based on each of these approaches are the same.

The plot that SPSS created is an effective way to illustrate the mean differences. You may want to edit the graph using what you learned in Chapter 3 to make it more elegant. Some people would prefer a bar chart since these are independent groups and a line suggests they are related. You could create a bar chart of these group means yourself.

Let's re-run the same analysis using the General Linear Model (GLM) and see how they are similar and different.

General Linear Model to Calculate One-Way ANOVAs

The Univariate General Linear Model is really intended to test models in which there is one dependent variable and multiple independent variables. We can use it to run a simple one-way ANOVA like the one above. One advantage of doing so is that we can estimate effect size from this menu, but we could not from the One-Way ANOVA menus. Let's try it.

✔ Select **Analyze/General Linear Model/Univariate**.

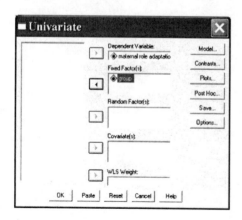

✔ As you can see by this dialog box, there are many more options than the One-Way ANOVA. This is because the GLM is a powerful technique that can examine complex designs. We'll just focus on what is relevant to us. As before, select maternal role adaptation as the **Dependent Variable** and group as the **Fixed Factor** or independent variable. Then, click **Plots**.

✔ Select group for the **Horizontal Axis** (X axis), and click add. Since there is only one dependent variable, SPSS knows that maternal role adaptation is on the Y axis without us needing the specify this. Click **Continue**.

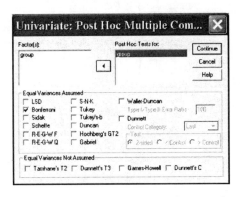

✔ Since this procedure can be used with multiple independent variables, we need to specify which ones to run post hoc comparisons for even though there is only one in our design. Select group for **Post Hoc Tests for**. This time, let's select **Bonferroni** to see if it makes a difference.

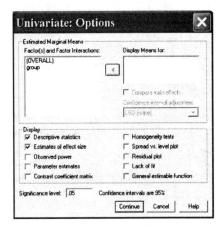

✔ Under **Display**, select **Descriptive statistics** and **Estimates of effect size**. Then click **Continue**. In the main dialog box, click **Ok**. The output follows.

Univariate Analysis of Variance

Between-Subjects Factors

		Value Label	N
GROUP	1.000	LBW Experimental	29
	2.000	LBW Control	27
	3.000	Full-term	37

Descriptive Statistics

Dependent Variable: maternal role adaptation (low sores better)

GROUP	Mean	Std. Deviation	N
LBW Experimental	14.96552	4.84387	29
LBW Control	18.33333	5.16646	27
Full-term	14.83784	3.70820	37
Total	15.89247	4.74677	93

Tests of Between-Subjects Effects

Dependent Variable: maternal role adaptation (low sores better)

Source	Type III Sum of Squares	df	Mean Square	F	Sig.	Eta Squared
Corrected Model	226.932[a]	2	113.466	5.532	.005	.109
Intercept	23513.095	1	23513.095	1146.364	.000	.927
GROUP	226.932	2	113.466	5.532	.005	.109
Error	1845.993	90	20.511			
Total	25562.000	93				
Corrected Total	2072.925	92				

a. R Squared = .109 (Adjusted R Squared = .090)

Post Hoc Tests

Multiple Comparisons

Dependent Variable: maternal role adaptation (low sores better)

Bonferroni

(I) GROUP	(J) GROUP	Mean Difference (I-J)	Std. Error	Sig.	95% Confidence Interval	
					Lower Bound	Upper Bound
LBW Experimental	LBW Control	-3.36782*	1.21117	.020	-6.32254	-.41309
	Full-term	.12768	1.12322	1.000	-2.61248	2.86784
LBW Control	LBW Experimental	3.36782*	1.21117	.020	.41309	6.32254
	Full-term	3.49550*	1.14631	.009	.69902	6.29197
Full-term	LBW Experimental	-.12768	1.12322	1.000	-2.86784	2.61248
	LBW Control	-3.49550*	1.14631	.009	-6.29197	-.69902

Based on observed means.

*. The mean difference is significant at the .05 level.

Profile Plots

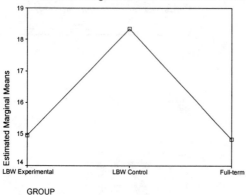

Estimated Marginal Means of maternal role ada

✔ Compare this output to the output from the One-Way ANOVA and the results in the textbook.

One difference is the appearance of the ANOVA summary table. Now, there is a row labeled intercept and another labeled adjusted. You can ignore these. The F value for Group is still the same, and that is what we are interested in. Notice the eta squared column. What does it say for group? Does this value agree with the textbook? Unfortunately SPSS does not calculate Omega squared, so you would have to do this by hand. Did the Bonferroni and the previous LSD multiple comparisons yield the same results?

You could edit any of the tables and graphs to look more elegant. For example, the current title of the graph is cut off. You would probably want to name it something else or use two lines of text. Editing the output would be ideal if you wanted to include your output in a paper. Use what you learned in Chapters 3 and 4 of this Manual to do so.

You can also calculate a one-way ANOVA and eta squared by using **Analyze/Compare Means/Means**. If you click on **Options**, you can select **ANOVA table and eta squared**. Try it yourself if you are interested. You will see that this menu does not allow you to run multiple comparisons, which is of course desired if you have more than 2 groups.

In this chapter, you learned 3 methods to calculate a One-Way ANOVA. I prefer the General Linear Model approach since this is the only one that gives us the option of calculating multiple comparisons and eta squared. Of course, you may feel otherwise depending on the information you wish to calculate. Complete the following exercises.

Exercises

Each of these exercises is based on *Eysenck recall.sav*. This study is presented in section 16.1 in the textbook.

1. Use ANOVA to compare the means. Select a post hoc procedure of your choice. Summarize the results.

2. Edit the ANOVA summary table so that it is suitable for inclusion in a paper.

3. Use SPSS to calculate eta squared. Note, how did you do this?

4. Create a bar chart to illustrate the differences between groups.

9. Comparing Means Using Factorial ANOVA

Objectives

- ◆Examine main effects and interactive effects
- ◆Calculate effect size
- ◆Calculate multiple comparisons for main effects
- ◆Calculate simple effects for interactive effects
- ◆Display means graphically

Factorial ANOVA using GLM Univariate

A Factorial ANOVA is an analysis of variance that includes more than one independent variable and calculates main effects for each independent variable and calculates interactive effects between independent variables. To calculate Factorial ANOVAs in SPSS we will use the General Linear Model again. Let's try an example together. We will use the extension of the Eysenck study described in the textbook in Sections 17.1 and 17.2. Now there are 2 independent variables, condition and age, being considered in relation to the dependent variable, recall.

✔ **Open** *Eysenck recall factorial.sav*.

✔ Select **Analyze/General Linear Model/Univariate**. Univariate means there is only one dependent variable.

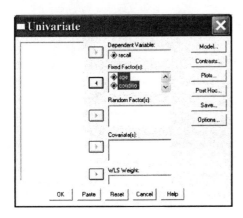

✔ Select recall as the **Dependent Variable**. Select age and condition as the **Fixed Factors** or independent variables. Then click on **Plots**.

✔ Since we are testing 3 effects, 2 main and one interactive, we may want to display 3 different graphs. First, select age for the **Horizontal Axis** and click **Add**. Then, select condition for the **Horizontal Axis** and click **Add**. Finally, select condition as the **Horizontal Axis** and age for **Separate Lines** to illustrate any interactive effect. I want to organize the interactive graph this way because I think it will be easier to interpret 2 lines representing the age groups than 5 separate lines representing the conditions. Click **Continue**.

✔ Click on **Post Hoc**. Since age only has 2 levels, there is no need to calculate multiple comparisons. If the effect is significant it can only mean the older and younger groups differ. Condition has 5 levels, so select it in **Post Hoc Tests for**. Select **LSD** as the procedure. Then, click **Continue**.

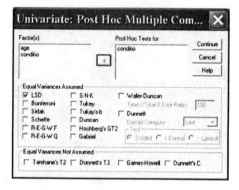

✔ Click **Options**. Select **Descriptive Statistics** and **Estimates of Effect Size** under **Display**. Then, click **Continue**, and finally, **Ok**. The output follows.

Univariate Analysis of Variance

Between-Subjects Factors

		Value Label	N
AGE	1	Older	50
	2	Younger	50
CONDITIO	1	Counting	20
	2	Rhyming	20
	3	Adjective	20
	4	Imagery	20
	5	Intentional	20

Descriptive Statistics

Dependent Variable: RECALL

AGE	CONDITIO	Mean	Std. Deviation	N
Older	Counting	7.00	1.83	10
	Rhyming	6.90	2.13	10
	Adjective	11.00	2.49	10
	Imagery	13.40	4.50	10
	Intentional	12.00	3.74	10
	Total	10.06	4.01	50
Younger	Counting	6.50	1.43	10
	Rhyming	7.60	1.96	10
	Adjective	14.80	3.49	10
	Imagery	17.60	2.59	10
	Intentional	19.30	2.67	10
	Total	13.16	5.79	50
Total	Counting	6.75	1.62	20
	Rhyming	7.25	2.02	20
	Adjective	12.90	3.54	20
	Imagery	15.50	4.17	20
	Intentional	15.65	4.90	20
	Total	11.61	5.19	100

Tests of Between-Subjects Effects

Dependent Variable: RECALL

Source	Type III Sum of Squares	df	Mean Square	F	Sig.	Eta Squared
Corrected Model	1945.490[a]	9	216.166	26.935	.000	.729
Intercept	13479.210	1	13479.210	1679.536	.000	.949
AGE	240.250	1	240.250	29.936	.000	.250
CONDITIO	1514.940	4	378.735	47.191	.000	.677
AGE * CONDITIO	190.300	4	47.575	5.928	.000	.209
Error	722.300	90	8.026			
Total	16147.000	100				
Corrected Total	2667.790	99				

a. R Squared = .729 (Adjusted R Squared = .702)

Post Hoc Tests

Multiple Comparisons

Dependent Variable: RECALL

LSD

(I) CONDITIO	(J) CONDITIO	Mean Difference (I-J)	Std. Error	Sig.	95% Confidence Interval	
					Lower Bound	Upper Bound
Counting	Rhyming	-.50	.90	.578	-2.28	1.28
	Adjective	-6.15*	.90	.000	-7.93	-4.37
	Imagery	-8.75*	.90	.000	-10.53	-6.97
	Intentional	-8.90*	.90	.000	-10.68	-7.12
Rhyming	Counting	.50	.90	.578	-1.28	2.28
	Adjective	-5.65*	.90	.000	-7.43	-3.87
	Imagery	-8.25*	.90	.000	-10.03	-6.47
	Intentional	-8.40*	.90	.000	-10.18	-6.62
Adjective	Counting	6.15*	.90	.000	4.37	7.93
	Rhyming	5.65*	.90	.000	3.87	7.43
	Imagery	-2.60*	.90	.005	-4.38	-.82
	Intentional	-2.75*	.90	.003	-4.53	-.97
Imagery	Counting	8.75*	.90	.000	6.97	10.53
	Rhyming	8.25*	.90	.000	6.47	10.03
	Adjective	2.60*	.90	.005	.82	4.38
	Intentional	-.15	.90	.867	-1.93	1.63
Intentional	Counting	8.90*	.90	.000	7.12	10.68
	Rhyming	8.40*	.90	.000	6.62	10.18
	Adjective	2.75*	.90	.003	.97	4.53
	Imagery	.15	.90	.867	-1.63	1.93

Based on observed means.

*. The mean difference is significant at the .05 level.

Profile Plots

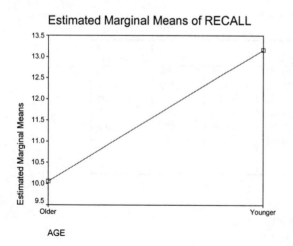

Estimated Marginal Means of RECALL

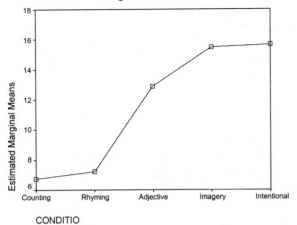

CONDITIO

Estimated Marginal Means of RECALL

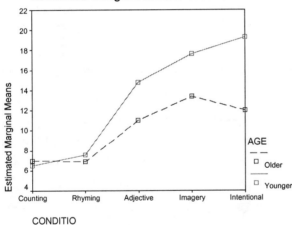

CONDITIO

✔ Compare this output to the results presented in the textbook in Table 17.3 and Figure 17.1.

As you can see, these results are in agreement. However, this is not the case for effect size. The reason is that SPSS calculates partial eta squared which is different than the computation in the textbook. SPSS uses the following equation:

$$\frac{SS_A}{SS_{error} + SS_A}$$ where A refers to an independent variable. The result will be the

same as eta squared if there is only one independent variable because the denominator would equal SS_{total}, but will differ when there are multiple independent variables. That explains why the eta squared calculated in the previous chapter was in agreement with the value in the textbook. This leaves us with 3 options: either report the adjusted eta squared, figure out another way to calculate eta squared with SPSS, or calculate eta squared by hand. You should probably ask your instructor whether or not it is OK to report the adjusted values. You can use **Compare Means/Means** to calculate eta squared for the main effects. See if you can remember how.

✔ Select **Analyze/Compare Means/Means**. Select recall for the **Dependent List**, and age and condition in Layer 1 of the **Independent List**. Click **Options** and select **ANOVA table and eta**. Click **Continue** and **Ok**. Just the relevant output is displayed below.

Measures of Association

	Eta	Eta Squared
RECALL * AGE	.300	.090

Measures of Association

	Eta	Eta Squared
RECALL * CONDITIO	.754	.568

As you can see, these values agree with those in the textbook for age and condition. You would still need to calculate eta squared for the interaction between age and condition.

Simple Effects

Now that we know there is a significant interaction between age and condition, we need to calculate the simple effects to help us interpret the interaction. The easiest way to do this is to split the file using the **Data/Split File** menu selections. Then, we can re-run the ANOVA testing the effects one independent variable on the dependent variable at each level of the other independent variable. For example, we can see the effect of condition on recall for younger participants and older participants. Because we will most likely wish to run our significance test using MS_{error} from the overall ANOVA, we will have to perform some hand calculations. After we get the new MS values for condition in each group, we will need to divide them by MS_{error} from the original analysis as noted in Table 17.3 of the textbook.

✔ In Data Editor View, click on **Data/Split file**.

✔ Select **Organize output by groups,** and select age for **Groups Based on.** Then, click **Ok**.

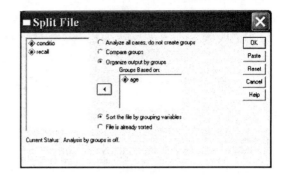

✔ Now, we are going to calculate the effect of condition on recall for each age group, so select **Analyze/Compare Means/One-Way ANOVA**.

✔ Select recall as the **Dependent Variable** and condition as the **Factor**. Then click **Continue**. There is no need to use Options to calculate means or create plots since we already did that when we ran the factorial ANOVA. So, click **Ok**. The output follows.

Oneway

AGE = Older

ANOVA[a]

RECALL

	Sum of Squares	df	Mean Square	F	Sig.
Between Groups	351.520	4	87.880	9.085	.000
Within Groups	435.300	45	9.673		
Total	786.820	49			

a. AGE = Older

AGE = Younger

ANOVA[a]

RECALL

	Sum of Squares	df	Mean Square	F	Sig.
Between Groups	1353.720	4	338.430	53.064	.000
Within Groups	287.000	45	6.378		
Total	1640.720	49			

a. AGE = Younger

✔ Compare MS$_{condition}$ (between groups) in the above tables to those presented in Table 17.4 of the book. As you can see, they are in agreement. Now, divide them by the MS$_{error}$ from the original ANOVA, 8.026. The calculations follow.

$$F_{\text{conditions at old}} = \frac{87.88}{8.026} = 10.95 \qquad F_{\text{conditions at young}} = \frac{338.43}{8.026} = 42.15$$

Thus, we end up with the same results. Although we had to perform some hand calculations, having SPSS calculate the mean square for conditions for us certainly simplifies things.

In this chapter you learned to calculate Factorial ANOVAs using GLM Univariate. In addition, you learned a shortcut to assist in calculating simple effects. Complete the following exercises to better familiarize yourself with these commands and options.

Exercises

1. Using *Eysenck factorial.sav*, calculate the simple effects for age at various conditions and compare them to the data in Table 17.4. [Hint: Split the file by condition now, and run the ANOVA with age as the independent variable.]

2. Use the data in *adaptation factorial.sav* to run a factorial ANOVA where group and education are the independent variables and maternal role adaptation is the dependent variable. Compare your results to Table 17.5 in the textbook.

3. Create a graph that illustrates the lack of an interactive effect between education and group on adaptation from the previous exercise.

10. Comparing Means Using Repeated Measures ANOVA

Objectives

- ♦ Calculate repeated measures ANOVAs
- ♦ Calculate effect size
- ♦ Conduct multiple comparisons
- ♦ Graphically illustrate mean differences

Repeated measures ANOVAs are used to examine mean differences in related variables. Typically the independent variable is either time (e.g., depression is measured in the same group of people at multiple points in time) or condition (e.g., each subject receives every condition). In SPSS, we will use the General Linear Model to calculate repeated measures ANOVAs.

Using GLM Repeated Measures to Calculate Repeated Measures ANOVAs

Let's begin with an example from the textbook illustrated in Section 18.1. In this example, the duration of migraine headaches was recorded among the same group of individuals over 5 weeks. The first 2 weeks were part of a baseline period and the final 3 weeks were part of an intervention period in which subjects were trained to apply relaxation techniques. In this case, the independent variable is time and the dependent variable is headache duration.

✓ **Open** *migraines.sav*.

✓ Select **Analyze/General Linear Model/Repeated Measures**.

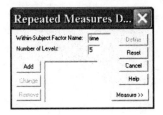

✓ The default for **Within-Subject Factor Name** is Factor 1. Let's change it to time by typing in the box. Specify 5 for **Number of Levels** since there are 5 weeks and then click **Add**. Next, click **Define**.

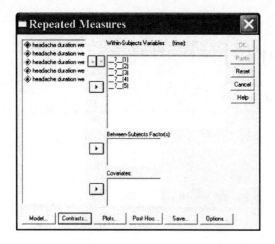

✔ As you can see, there are 5 spots under **Within-Subject Variables**. We need to indicate that each week is a variable, and we want to list them in the right order. You can either select them one at a time and arrow them into the variable list, or you can select them all by holding down the control button while you select each one, and arrow them in at once. This is a simple design, so there are no Between-Subject Factors or Covariates. Click **Plots**.

✔ Select time as the **Horizontal Axis** or Y Axis. Then click **Add**, and **Continue**. This will plot the mean duration of headaches for each week for us. In the main dialog box, click **Options**.

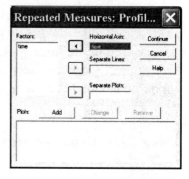

✔ Under **Display**, select **Descriptive Statistics**, **Estimates of Effect Size**, and **Observed Power**. Then click **Continue**. And finally, **Ok**. The output follows.

General Linear Model

Within-Subjects Factors

Measure: MEASURE_1

TIME	Dependent Variable
1	WEEK1
2	WEEK2
3	WEEK3
4	WEEK4
5	WEEK5

Descriptive Statistics

	Mean	Std. Deviation	N
headache duration week 1	20.78	7.17	9
headache duration week 2	20.00	10.22	9
headache duration week 3	9.00	3.12	9
headache duration week 4	5.78	3.42	9
headache duration week 5	6.78	4.12	9

Multivariate Tests[c]

Effect		Value	F	Hypothesis df	Error df	Sig.	Eta Squared	Noncent. Parameter	Observed Power[a]
TIME	Pillai's Trace	.909	12.548[b]	4.000	5.000	.008	.909	50.191	.952
	Wilks' Lambda	.091	12.548[b]	4.000	5.000	.008	.909	50.191	.952
	Hotelling's Trace	10.038	12.548[b]	4.000	5.000	.008	.909	50.191	.952
	Roy's Largest Root	10.038	12.548[b]	4.000	5.000	.008	.909	50.191	.952

a. Computed using alpha = .05

b. Exact statistic

c.
    Design: Intercept
    Within Subjects Design: TIME

Mauchly's Test of Sphericity[b]

Measure: MEASURE_1

					Epsilon[a]		
Within Subjects Effect	Mauchly's W	Approx. Chi-Square	df	Sig.	Greenhouse-Geisser	Huynh-Feldt	Lower-bound
TIME	.030	22.516	9	.009	.422	.522	.250

Tests the null hypothesis that the error covariance matrix of the orthonormalized transformed dependent variables is proportional to an identity matrix.

a. May be used to adjust the degrees of freedom for the averaged tests of significance. Corrected tests are displayed in the Tests of Within-Subjects Effects table.

b.
    Design: Intercept
    Within Subjects Design: TIME

Tests of Within-Subjects Effects

Measure: MEASURE_1

Source		Type III Sum of Squares	df	Mean Square	F	Sig.	Eta Squared	Noncent. Parameter	Observed Power[a]
TIME	Sphericity Assumed	1934.533	4	483.633	21.463	.000	.728	85.852	1.000
	Greenhouse-Geisser	1934.533	1.687	1146.534	21.463	.000	.728	36.214	.999
	Huynh-Feldt	1934.533	2.089	926.174	21.463	.000	.728	44.831	1.000
	Lower-bound	1934.533	1.000	1934.533	21.463	.002	.728	21.463	.981
Error(TIME)	Sphericity Assumed	721.067	32	22.533					
	Greenhouse-Geisser	721.067	13.498	53.419					
	Huynh-Feldt	721.067	16.710	43.152					
	Lower-bound	721.067	8.000	90.133					

a. Computed using alpha = .05

Tests of Within-Subjects Contrasts

Measure: MEASURE_1

Source	TIME	Type III Sum of Squares	df	Mean Square	F	Sig.	Eta Squared	Noncent. Parameter	Observed Power[a]
TIME	Linear	1604.444	1	1604.444	36.181	.000	.819	36.181	.999
	Quadratic	82.571	1	82.571	6.215	.037	.437	6.215	.591
	Cubic	187.778	1	187.778	17.066	.003	.681	17.066	.950
	Order 4	59.740	1	59.740	2.779	.134	.258	2.779	.312
Error(TIME)	Linear	354.756	8	44.344					
	Quadratic	106.286	8	13.286					
	Cubic	88.022	8	11.003					
	Order 4	172.003	8	21.500					

a. Computed using alpha = .05

Tests of Between-Subjects Effects

Measure: MEASURE_1

Transformed Variable: Average

Source	Type III Sum of Squares	df	Mean Square	F	Sig.	Eta Squared	Noncent. Parameter	Observed Power[a]
Intercept	6993.800	1	6993.800	67.119	.000	.894	67.119	1.000
Error	833.600	8	104.200					

a. Computed using alpha = .05

Profile Plots

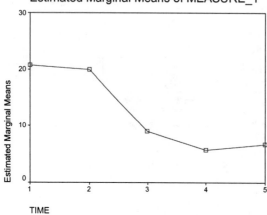

Estimated Marginal Means of MEASURE_1

As you can see, there is a lot of output, much of which we can ignore for our purposes. Specifically, ignore Multivariate Tests, Tests of Within-Subjects Contrasts, and Tests of Between Subjects Effects. Now, let's look at the rest and compare it to the Table 18.1 in the textbook. First, you can compare the mean scores for each week by looking at the **Descriptive Statistics** table. The next piece is **Mauchly's Test of Sphericity**, which tests the assumption that each of the time periods is approximately equally correlated with every other score. As noted in the text, when this assumption is violated, various corrections are applied. The next table of interest, **Tests of Within-Subjects Effects** is what we really want to see. Compare the textbook values to those listed in the rows marked Sphericity Assumed, because they were calculated the same way. As you can see, they are in agreement.

Now, note the values for eta squared and observed power. Can you interpret them? Nearly 73% of the variability in headache duration is accounted for by time. Observed power is based on the assumption that the true difference in population means is the difference implied by the sample means. Typically, we want to calculate power going into an experiment based on anticipated or previous effect size in other similar studies. This is useful in making decisions about sample size. So, observed power calculated here is not particularly useful.

The graph is a nice illustration of the mean headache duration over time. You may want to edit it to include more meaningful labels and a title.

Now, we need to calculate multiple comparisons to help us understand the meaning of the significant effect of time on headache duration.

Multiple Comparisons

Let's just try one of the multiple comparisons calculated in the book, the comparison between the overall baseline mean and the overall training mean. We can use SPSS Transform/Compute to calculate these averages for us rather than doing it manually.

✔ In the Data Editor window, select **Transform/Compute**.

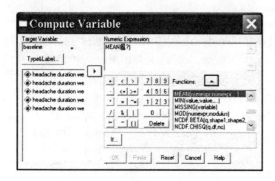

✔ Type baseline under **Target Variable**. The under the list of **Functions**, select **MEAN** and arrow it into the dialog box. We need to tell SPSS from what variables to calculate the mean. Select week1 and week2 to replace the 2 question marks. Make sure they are separated by a comma and the question marks are gone. Then, click **Ok**.

✔ Look at the new variable in the Data Editor. Does it look right?

✔ Click **Transform/Compute** again. Click **Reset** to remove the previous information. Name the next **Target Variable** training. Select **MEAN** again. Specify, week3, week4, and week5. Make sure the question marks are gone and commas separate each variable. Then, click **Ok**. Check out your new variable.

✔ Use **Analyze/Descriptives** to calculate the means for baseline and training. The data follow.

Descriptives

Descriptive Statistics

	N	Minimum	Maximum	Mean	Std. Deviation
BASELINE	9	6.00	31.50	20.3889	8.3133
TRAINING	9	4.00	13.00	7.1852	2.8437
Valid N (listwise)	9				

As you can see, the means are consistent with those reported in the textbook. Now, you can apply formula using MS_{error} from the ANOVA. The computations follow.

$$t = \frac{20.39 - 7.17}{\sqrt{22.53(\frac{1}{18} + \frac{1}{27})}} = \frac{13.20}{\sqrt{2.086}} = 9.14$$

Although some hand calculations are required, we saved time and reduced the likelihood of making errors by using SPSS to compute the new mean scores for baseline and training for us.

In this chapter, you learned to use the General Linear Model to calculate repeated measures ANOVAs. In addition, you learned to use SPSS to calculate new means for use in multiple comparisons. Try the following exercises to help you become more familiar with the process.

Exercises

The following exercises are based on *Eysenck repeated.sav*.

1. Use a repeated measures ANOVA to examine the effect of condition on recall. Compare your results to those presented in the textbook in Section 18.7.

2. Use SPSS to calculate the effect size of condition.

3. Plot the mean difference in recall by conditions.

4. Use SPSS to calculate the mean of counting, rhyming, adjective, and intentional and label it lowproc for lower processing. Then use the multiple comparisons procedure explained in the textbook to compare the mean recall from the lower processing conditions to the mean recall for imagery, which was the highest processing condition. Write a brief statement explaining the results.

11. Chi Square

Objectives

 ◆ Calculate goodness of fit Chi Square
 ◆ Calculate Chi Square for contingency tables
 ◆ Calculate effect size
 ◆ Save data entry time by weighting cases

A Chi Square is used to analyze categorical data. It compares observed frequencies to expected or predicted frequencies. We will examine simple goodness of fit Chi Squares that involved only one variable and more complicated contingency tables that include 2 or more variables. Each type is programmed through different menu options. Let's start with goodness of fit.

Goodness of Fit Chi Square All Categories Equal

Let's begin by using the example in Section 19.1 of the text. We want to test the null hypothesis that rats are equally likely to choose Alley A and Alley B when trying to escape.

 ✔ **Open** *alley chosen.sav*.

 ✔ Select **Analyze/Nonparametric Tests/Chi Square**.

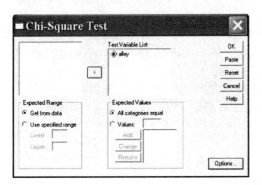

 ✔ Select alley as the **Test Variable**. Under **Expected Values**, All categories equal is the default. This is what we want since our null hypothesis is that each alley is equally likely to be chosen. Click **Ok**. The output follows.

99

Chi-Square Test

Frequencies

ALLEY

	Observed N	Expected N	Residual
A	9	16.0	-7.0
B	23	16.0	7.0
Total	32		

Test Statistics

	ALLEY
Chi-Square[a]	6.125
df	1
Asymp. Sig.	.013

a. 0 cells (.0%) have expected frequencies less than 5. The minimum expected cell frequency is 16.0.

As you can see, the expected values were 16 each, just as we expected. Now, compare this Chi Square to the value computed in Section 19.1 of the textbook. Once again, they are in agreement.

Goodness of Fit Chi Square Categories Unequal

Now, let's try an example where the expected values are not equal across categories. The difference is we have to specify the expected proportions. This example is based on Exercise 19.3 in the textbook, but the numbers in the data set are slightly different. In the exercise, Howell discusses his theory that when asked to sort one-sentence characteristics like "I eat too fast" into piles ranging from "not at all like me" to "very much like me," the percentage of items placed in each pile will be approximately 10%, 20%, 40%, 20%, and 10%. In our data set, the frequencies are 7, 11, 21,7, and 4 respectively.

✔ **Open** *unequal categories.sav*. There is no need to save *alley chosen.sav* since we did not change the data file in anyway.

✔ Select **Analyze/Nonparametric Statistics/Chi Square**.

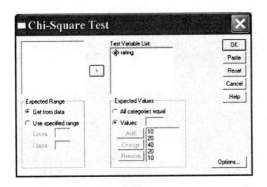

✔ Select rating as the **Test Variable**. Under **Expected Values**, select **Values**. Now, we have to type in the expected *proportion* of cases that should fit each category. These must be specified in order to match the ascending numeric order of the categories in our data files (e.g., 1 = not at all like to 5 = very much like). So, type 10, click **Add**. Type **20**, click **Add**, etc. Then, click **Ok**. The output follows.

Chi-Square Test

Frequencies

RATING

	Observed N	Expected N	Residual
not at all like me	7	5.0	2.0
somewhat unlike me	11	10.0	1.0
neither like me or unlike me	21	20.0	1.0
somewhat like me	7	10.0	-3.0
very much like me	4	5.0	-1.0
Total	50		

Test Statistics

	RATING
Chi-Square[a]	2.050
df	4
Asymp. Sig.	.727

a. 0 cells (.0%) have expected frequencies less than 5. The minimum expected cell frequency is 5.0.

As you can see, SPSS calculated the expected values based on the proportions that we indicated-check the math if you would like. In this case, the fact that the Chi Square is not significant supports the hypothesis. The observed frequencies of ratings fit with the predicted frequencies.

Chi Square for Contingency Tables

Let's use the example illustrated in Section 19.2 of the textbook. We want to examine the hypothesis that perceived fault of a rape victim is related to whether or not the defendant is found guilty.

As you can see the data are nicely displayed in a table in the textbook. This is a great opportunity to show you a nifty trick called weighting cases. Essentially, this will allow us to get SPSS to analyze the data presented in the textbook, without having to enter 358 pieces of data!

✔ Select **File/New/Data**.

✔ In Variable View, create two variables. **Name** one fault and specify the **Values** such that 1 = low fault and 2 = high fault. **Name** the other variable verdict and specify the **Values** such that 1= guilty and 2 = not guilty. Then return to the Data View.

✔ There are four possible combinations of the two variables, as illustrated in the textbook. They are low fault/guilty, low fault/not guilty, high fault/guilty, and high fault/not guilty. So, enter 1,1,2, 2 under fault and 1, 2, 1, 2 under verdict, in the first four rows. A sample follows.

	fault	verdict
1	1.00	1.00
2	1.00	2.00
3	2.00	1.00
4	2.00	2.00

✔ Now, we need to indicate the frequencies for each combination. Create a new variable and **Name** it counts. Then enter the appropriate frequencies for each combination. A sample follows-this time, I will display it with the variable labels on so it is similar to the table in the textbook.

	fault	verdict	counts
1	low fault	guilty	153.00
2	low fault	not guilty	24.00
3	high fault	guilty	105.00
4	high fault	not guilty	76.00

✔ Select **Data/Weight Cases**.

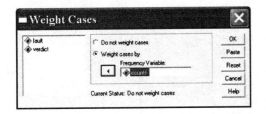

✔ Select **Weight cases by** and select counts as the **Frequency Variable**. Click **Ok**. Until we turn this off, SPSS will run analyses based on the frequencies we have specified here.

✔ Select **Analyze/Descriptive Statistics/Crosstabs**.

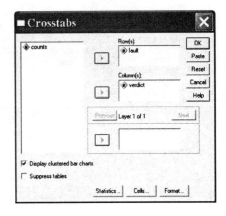

✔ To be consistent with the presentation in the textbook, select fault for **Rows** and verdict for **Columns**. Select **Display clustered bar charts** to help us visualize the data. Click on **Statistics**.

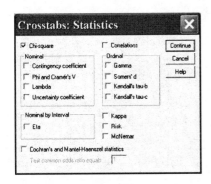

✔ Select **Chi-square**, and then click **Continue**. Under **Nominal**, select **Phi and Cramer's V** as well so we can get a measure of effect size. In the main dialog box, click on **Cells**.

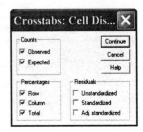

✔ Under **Count**, select **Observed** and **Expected**. Under **Percentages**, select **Row**, **Column**, and **Total**. Then click **Continue**. In the main dialog box, click **Ok**. The output follows.

Crosstabs

Case Processing Summary

	Cases					
	Valid		Missing		Total	
	N	Percent	N	Percent	N	Percent
FAULT * VERDICT	358	100.0%	0	.0%	358	100.0%

FAULT * VERDICT Crosstabulation

			VERDICT		Total
			guilty	not guilty	
FAULT	low fault	Count	153	24	177
		Expected Count	127.6	49.4	177.0
		% within FAULT	86.4%	13.6%	100.0%
		% within VERDICT	59.3%	24.0%	49.4%
		% of Total	42.7%	6.7%	49.4%
	high fault	Count	105	76	181
		Expected Count	130.4	50.6	181.0
		% within FAULT	58.0%	42.0%	100.0%
		% within VERDICT	40.7%	76.0%	50.6%
		% of Total	29.3%	21.2%	50.6%
Total		Count	258	100	358
		Expected Count	258.0	100.0	358.0
		% within FAULT	72.1%	27.9%	100.0%
		% within VERDICT	100.0%	100.0%	100.0%
		% of Total	72.1%	27.9%	100.0%

Chi-Square Tests

	Value	df	Asymp. Sig. (2-sided)	Exact Sig. (2-sided)	Exact Sig. (1-sided)
Pearson Chi-Square	35.930[b]	1	.000		
Continuity Correction[a]	34.532	1	.000		
Likelihood Ratio	37.351	1	.000		
Fisher's Exact Test				.000	.000
Linear-by-Linear Association	35.830	1	.000		
N of Valid Cases	358				

a. Computed only for a 2x2 table

b. 0 cells (.0%) have expected count less than 5. The minimum expected count is 49.44.

Symmetric Measures

		Value	Approx. Sig.
Nominal by Nominal	Phi	.317	.000
	Cramer's V	.317	.000
N of Valid Cases		358	

a. Not assuming the null hypothes is.

b. Using the asymptotic standard error as suming the null hypothes is.

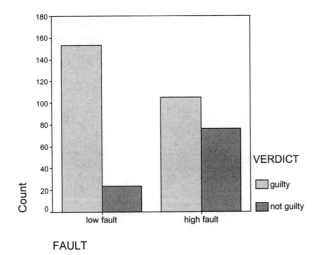

FAULT

The first thing to notice is that in the table named **Case Processing Summary**, the N is 358. This demonstrates that weighting cases worked as we intended! Now compare the Expected Counts to the values in the text. Finally, compare the Chi Square values. We are interested in the Pearson Chi Square because it was calculated the same way as the one in the textbook. Once again, the results are consistent with the textbook.

In this chapter you learned to use SPSS to calculate Goodness of Fit tests with and without equal frequencies. You also learned to calculate Chi Square for contingency tables, and learned a trick to reduce data entry by weighting cases. Complete the following exercises to help you become familiar with these commands.

Exercises

1. Using *alley chosen multi.sav,* use a Goodness of Fit Chi Square to test the hypothesis that rats are more likely than chance to choose Alley D. Compare your results to Section 19.1, Extension of the Multicategory Case, in the textbook.

2. Solve Exercise 19.3 from the textbook using SPSS. The data are in *Exercise 19.3.sav.*

3. Create your own data file to represent the observed data presented in the textbook in Table 19.2 using Weight Cases.

4. Using the data file you created in Exercise 3, calculate a Chi Square using crosstabs to examine the hypothesis that the number of bystanders is related to seeking assistance. Be sure to calculate Cramer's Phi. Compare your results to the textbook.

12. Nonparametric Statistics

Objectives

- ◆ Calculate Mann-Whitney Test
- ◆ Calculate Wilcoxon's Matched-Pairs Signed-Ranks Test
- ◆ Calculate Kruskal-Wallis One-Way ANOVA
- ◆ Calculate Friedman's Rank Test for k Correlated Samples

Nonparametric statistics or distribution-free tests are those that do not rely on parameter estimates or precise assumptions about the distributions of variables. In this chapter we will learn how to use SPSS Nonparametric statistics to compare 2 independent groups, 2 paired samples, k independent groups, and k related samples.

Mann-Whitney Test

Let's begin by comparing 2 independent groups using the Mann-Whitney Test. We'll use the example presented in Table 20.1 in the textbook. We want to compare the number of stressful life events reported by cardiac patients and orthopedic patients.

✔ **Open** *stressful events.sav.*

✔ Select **Analyze/Nonparametric Tests/Two Independent Samples**.

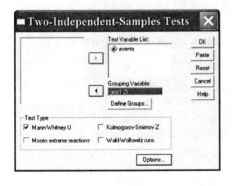

✔ Select events as the **Test Variable** and group as the **Grouping Variable**. Click on **Define Groups** and specify 1 for **Group 1** and 2 for **Group 2**, then click **Continue**. Under Test-Type, select **Mann-Whitney U**. Then click on **Options**.

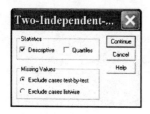

✔ Under **Statistics**, select **Descriptives**. Then click **Continue**. In the main dialog box, click **Ok**. The output follows.

NPar Tests

Descriptive Statistics

	N	Mean	Std. Deviation	Minimum	Maximum
EVENTS	11	8.64	11.12	0	32
GRP	11	1.45	.52	1	2

Mann-Whitney Test

Ranks

	GRP	N	Mean Rank	Sum of Ranks
EVENTS	1	6	7.50	45.00
	2	5	4.20	21.00
	Total	11		

Test Statistics[b]

	EVENTS
Mann-Whitney U	6.000
Wilcoxon W	21.000
Z	-1.647
Asymp. Sig. (2-tailed)	.100
Exact Sig. [2*(1-tailed Sig.)]	.126[a]

a. Not corrected for ties.

b. Grouping Variable: GRP

Compare this output to the results in Section 20.1 of the textbook. Specifically, focus on the row labeled Wilcoxon W in the **Test Statistics** table. As you can see they are the same. There is not a statistically significant difference in stressful life events for the 2 groups.

Wilcoxon's Matched Pairs Signed-Ranks Test

Now, let's compare paired or related data. We will use the example illustrated in Section 20.2 of the textbook. We will compare systolic blood pressure from before and after a training session.

✔ **Open** *blood pressure.sav*.

✔ Select **Analyze/Nonparametric Tests/2 Related Samples**.

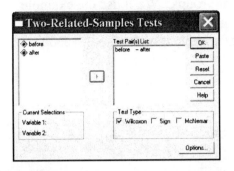

✔ Select before and after for the **Test Pairs List**. Select **Wilcoxon** for **Test Type**. Then, click **Ok**. The output follows.

NPar Tests

Wilcoxon Signed Ranks Test

Ranks

		N	Mean Rank	Sum of Ranks
AFTER - BEFORE	Negative Ranks	6ª	4.50	27.00
	Positive Ranks	2ᵇ	4.50	9.00
	Ties	0ᶜ		
	Total	8		

a. AFTER < BEFORE

b. AFTER > BEFORE

c. BEFORE = AFTER

Test Statisticsᵇ

	AFTER - BEFORE
Z	-1.260ª
Asymp. Sig. (2-tailed)	.208

a. Based on positive ranks.

b. Wilcoxon Signed Ranks Test

The Sum of Ranks column includes the T values. Compare them to the values in the textbook. Note that the test statistic in SPSS is Z. Regardless, the results are the same. There is not a significant difference in blood pressure at the two points in time.

Kruskal-Wallis One-Way ANOVA

Now let's compare more than 2 independent groups. We'll use the example illustrated in Table 20.4 of the textbook, comparing the number of problems solved correctly in one hour by people who received a depressant, stimulant, or placebo drug.

✔ **Open** *problem solving.sav.*

✔ Select **Analyze/Nonparametric Test/ K Independent Samples**.

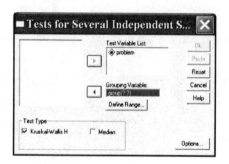

✔ Select problem as the **Test Variable** and group as the **Grouping Variable**. Then, click on **Define Range**.

✔ Indicate 1 for the **Minimum** and 3 for the **Maximum** since there are 3 groups, identified as 1,2, and 3. Click **Continue**.

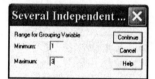

✔ Kruskal-Wallis is already selected in the main dialog box, so just click **Ok**. The output follows.

NPar Tests

Kruskal-Wallis Test

Ranks

	GROUP	N	Mean Rank
PROBLEM	1	7	5.00
	2	8	14.38
	3	4	10.00
	Total	19	

Test Statistics[a,b]

	PROBLEM
Chi-Square	10.407
df	2
Asymp. Sig.	.005

a. Kruskal Wallis Test

b. Grouping Variable: GROUP

As you can see these results agree with those in the text, with minor differences in the decimal places. This is due to rounding. Both sets of results support the conclusion that problems solved correctly varied significantly by group.

Friedman's Rank Test for K Related Samples

Now, let's move on to an example with K related samples. We'll use the data presented in Table 20.5 of the textbook as an example. We want to see if reading time is effected when reading pronouns that do not fit common gender stereotypes.

✔ **Open** *pronouns.sav*.

✔ Select **Analyze/Nonparametric Tests/K Related Samples**.

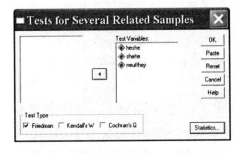

✔ Select heshe, shehe, and neuthey as the **Test Variables**. **Friedman** is the default for **Test Type**, so we can click **Ok**. The output follows.

Friedman Test

Ranks

	Mean Rank
HESHE	2.00
SHEHE	2.64
NEUTTHEY	1.36

Test Statistics[a]

N	11
Chi-Square	8.909
df	2
Asymp. Sig.	.012

a. Friedman Test

As you can see, the Chi Square value is in agreement with the one in the text. We can conclude that reading times are related to pronoun conditions.

In this chapter, you learned to use SPSS to calculate each of the Nonparametric Statistics included in the textbook. Complete the following exercises to help you become familiar with each.

Exercises

1. Using *birthweight.sav*, use the Mann-Whitney Test to compare the birthweight of babies born to mothers who began prenatal care in the third trimester to those who began prenatal classes in the first trimester. Compare your results to the results presented in Table 20.2 of the textbook. (Note: SPSS chooses to work with the sum of the scores in the *larger* group (71), and thus n_1 and n_2 are reversed. This will give you the same z score, with the sign reversed. Notice that z in the output agrees with z in the text.)

2. Using *anorexia family therapy.sav* (the same example used for the paired t-test in Chapter 7 of this manual), compare the subjects' weight pre and post intervention using Wilcoxon's Matched Pairs Signed Ranks Test. What can you conclude?

3. Using *maternal role adaptation.sav* (the same example used for one-way ANOVA in Chapter 8 of this manual), compare maternal role adaptation for the 3 groups of mothers using the Kruskal-Wallis ANOVA. What can you conclude?

4. Using *Eysenck recall repeated.sav* (the same example used for Repeated Measures ANOVA in Chapter 10 of this manual), examine the effect of processing condition on recall using Friedman's Test. What can you conclude?

Conclusion

In the beginning of this manual, you learned the basics of operating SPSS. Throughout the remainder of the manual, you saw examples to help you learn to use SPSS to calculate each of the statistics covered in Howell's Fundamental Statistics for the Behavioral Sciences, 5th edition. Using SPSS is much like using any other computer program. That is, your confidence and ease with the program will increase with exposure and practice. With that in mind, we encourage you to attempt to solve other problems using SPSS.

One of the lessons I hope you have learned from this manual is to explore the various options and subcommands built into SPSS. I only reviewed the ones relevant to the textbook. You may find other options useful for your own purposes, so I encourage you to explore them. Finally, remember to use Help. In fact, that is how I learned many of the tips and tricks discussed in this manual.

Answer Key for Exercises

Exercises-Chapter 1

1.1   A variety of topics appear under ANOVA. A summary is below. You should look at some of the topics in more detail.

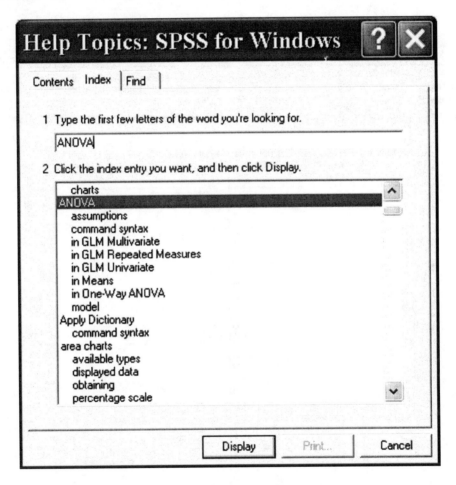

1.2   I found 2 sets of information: one for categorical or nominal data and another for continuous data. Clicking on either one gave me suggestions about appropriate types of analyses to run given these types of data.

1.3   This will change the view in the Data Editor. When it is checked each piece of data is in a cell (surrounded by lines), when it is not checked, the cells are not divided by lines.

1.4   This is a matter of personal preference. There is no right answer.

1.5   This is a matter of personal preference. There is no right answer.

Exercises-Chapter 2

2.1   A sample of labels and values follows.

Name	Type	Width	Decimals	Label	Values
trial	Numeric	5	0		None
rxtime	Numeric	6	0	reaction times in 100th of a second	None
nstim	Numeric	5	0	number of digits	None
yesno	Numeric	5	0	was test digit included in comparison set	{1, yes}...

2.2   A sample of the correct data file follows.

	intrus
1	0
2	1
3	1
4	2
5	2
6	3
7	4
8	4
9	4
10	5
11	5
12	5
13	6

2.3   Answers will vary depending on how you created your own data file. Remember to compare your file to *Exercise2.2.sav* on the CD.

2.4   To perform this exercise accurately, you would have used the merge/add cases option. The only way you would know this is by opening the 2 original files

116

and looking at them. You can see both include the same variables, but include the data from different people. The merged file will include 90 cases.

2.5   To do this effectively, you would need to have noticed that the variable names were included at the top of the file and that commas delimited the data. A sample of the correct data file follows.

	id	gender	q1	q2	q3
1	1.0	2	3	4	5
2	2.0	1	1	2	3
3	3.0	1	2	3	4
4	4.0	2	3	4	5
5	5.0	1	4	5	5
6	6.0	2	1	1	1
7	7.0	1	1	2	2
8	8.0	2	3	3	4
9	9.0	2	5	4	3
10	10.0	1	3	4	5
11	11.0	1	3	4	5

2.6   All of the original variable names were longer than 8 characters, so I renamed them before reading them into EXCEL so they wouldn't end up with generic or truncated names. A sample data file follows.

	name	group	tgrade1	tgrade2
1	Jennifer	1	90	88
2	Michelle	2	65	67
3	Moriah	1	78	85
4	Matthew	1	85	78
5	Jacob	2	87	84
6	John	2	67	65
7	Melissa	1	75	77
8	Casey	2	78	90
9	Corinne	1	89	877
10	Keith	1	92	94
11	Amanda	2	90	90

3.1   A histogram for ADDSC follows.

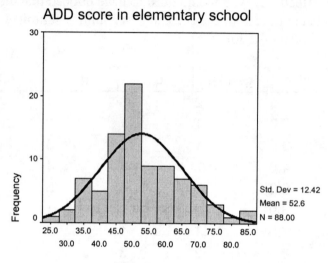

3.2   The box plots follow. It appears that students with social problems have more ADD symptoms than students without social problems. The distribution appears more normally distributed for students with no social problems. The distribution for students with social problems appears positively skewed. Neither group has outliers.

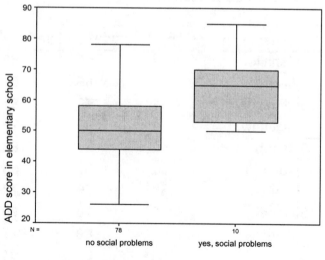

3.3   A sample scatter plot follows. There appears to be a negative association between GPA and ADD symptoms.

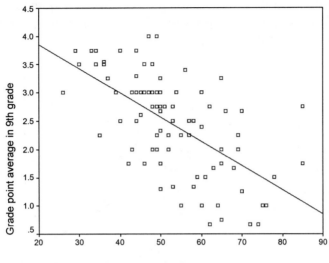

ADD score in elementary school

3.4   A sample bar chart follows. It looks as if GPA differs between the 3 groups such that students in the college prep course have higher GPAs than students in general or remedial English, and students in general English have higher GPAs than students in remedial English. [Of course, we would need to compute some inferential statistics to see if these differences are statistically significant.]

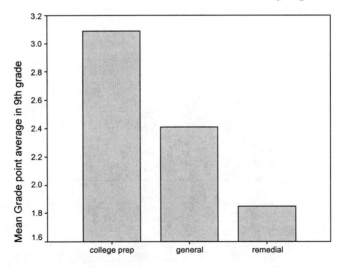

level of English in 9th grade

3.5   The 2 graphs follow. It looks like there is a main effect of type of English class as described above. It also looks like there is a main effect of gender such that females have higher GPAs than males. I would guess there is an interaction effect such that the gender difference in GPA is greatest among students in college prep English. I like the line graph better because I think it is easier to visualize interaction effects with a line graph than a bar graph.

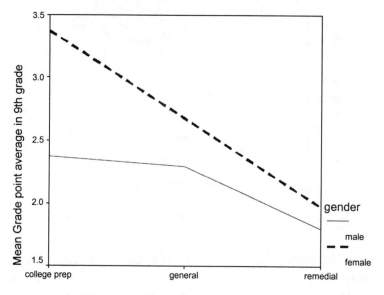

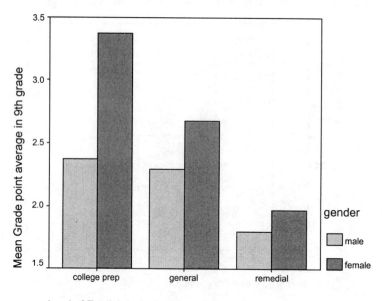

Exercises-Chapter 4

4.1   The output follows. I used Analyze/Descriptive Statistics/Frequencies to calculate these descriptives because it includes all of the options including the histogram.

Frequencies

Statistics

		self esteem	anxiety score	coping score	health score
N	Valid	50	48	50	50
	Missing	0	2	0	0
Mean		3.4933	3.8558	2.0856	3.0249
Median		3.6667	4.0000	1.9688	3.0000
Mode		4.00	3.50[a]	1.76[a]	3.00
Std. Deviation		.5139	.7337	.5570	.6146
Variance		.2641	.5383	.3102	.3777
Range		2.17	2.75	2.53	2.72

a. Multiple modes exist. The smallest value is shown

Histogram

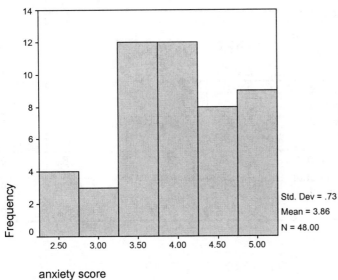

anxiety score

4.2   I calculated these frequencies using Analyze/Descriptive Statistics/Crosstabs.
The results follow.

gender * social problems in 9th grade Crosstabulation

			social problems in 9th grade		
			no social problems	yes, social problems	Total
gender	male	Count	48	7	55
		% within gender	87.3%	12.7%	100.0%
	female	Count	30	3	33
		% within gender	90.9%	9.1%	100.0%
Total		Count	78	10	88
		% within gender	88.6%	11.4%	100.0%

4.3   The output follows. I calculated them by using Analyze/Compare
Means/Means.

Report

Grade point average in 9th grade

social problems in	dropped out of	Mean	N	Std. Deviation	Variance
no social problems	did not drop out	2.5293	73	.8744	.764
	dropped out of high school	1.5340	5	.6171	.381
	Total	2.4655	78	.8915	.795
yes, social problems	did not drop out	2.3500	5	.8023	.644
	dropped out of high school	2.4180	5	.4218	.178
	Total	2.3840	10	.6054	.366
Total	did not drop out	2.5178	78	.8662	.750
	dropped out of high school	1.9760	10	.6822	.465
	Total	2.4562	88	.8614	.742

Exercises-Chapter 5

5.1   The two-tailed correlations follow. Using a one-tailed versus a two-tailed test did not matter in this case because all of the correlations are statistically significant at the p<.01 level. This would make a difference if correlation were marginally significant. For example, if a p value is .10 as a two-tailed test, it would be non-significant. The same correlation would be significant as a one-tailed test.

Correlations

		ADD score in elementary school	IQ score	Grade point average in 9th grade	grade in ninth grade English
ADD score in elementary school	Pearson Correlation	1.000	-.632**	-.615**	-.478**
	Sig. (2-tailed)	.	.000	.000	.000
	N	88	88	88	88
IQ score	Pearson Correlation	-.632**	1.000	.497**	.370**
	Sig. (2-tailed)	.000	.	.000	.000
	N	88	88	88	88
Grade point average in 9th grade	Pearson Correlation	-.615**	.497**	1.000	.839**
	Sig. (2-tailed)	.000	.000	.	.000
	N	88	88	88	88
grade in ninth grade English	Pearson Correlation	-.478**	.370**	.839**	1.000
	Sig. (2-tailed)	.000	.000	.000	.
	N	88	88	88	88

**. Correlation is significant at the 0.01 level (2-tailed).

5.2   The output follow. All of the correlations are quite different between the two groups accept the correlation between GPA and grade in 9th grade English, which correlate positively in both groups.

dropped out of high school = did not drop out

Correlations[a]

		ADD score in elementary school	IQ score	Grade point average in 9th grade	grade in ninth grade English
ADD score in elementary school	Pearson Correlation	1.000	-.614**	-.625**	-.493**
	Sig. (2-tailed)	.	.000	.000	.000
	N	78	78	78	78
IQ score	Pearson Correlation	-.614**	1.000	.491**	.365**
	Sig. (2-tailed)	.000	.	.000	.001
	N	78	78	78	78
Grade point average in 9th grade	Pearson Correlation	-.625**	.491**	1.000	.836**
	Sig. (2-tailed)	.000	.000	.	.000
	N	78	78	78	78
grade in ninth grade English	Pearson Correlation	-.493**	.365**	.836**	1.000
	Sig. (2-tailed)	.000	.001	.000	.
	N	78	78	78	78

**. Correlation is significant at the 0.01 level (2-tailed).

a. dropped out of high school = did not drop out

dropped out of high school = dropped out of high school

Correlations[a]

		ADD score in elementary school	IQ score	Grade point average in 9th grade	grade in ninth grade English
ADD score in elementary school	Pearson Correlation	1.000	-.137	-.216	.036
	Sig. (2-tailed)	.	.706	.548	.921
	N	10	10	10	10
IQ score	Pearson Correlation	-.137	1.000	.020	-.156
	Sig. (2-tailed)	.706	.	.955	.667
	N	10	10	10	10
Grade point average in 9th grade	Pearson Correlation	-.216	.020	1.000	.825**
	Sig. (2-tailed)	.548	.955	.	.003
	N	10	10	10	10
grade in ninth grade English	Pearson Correlation	.036	-.156	.825**	1.000
	Sig. (2-tailed)	.921	.667	.003	.
	N	10	10	10	10

**. Correlation is significant at the 0.01 level (2-tailed).

a. dropped out of high school = dropped out of high school

5.3   A sample scatter plot follows.

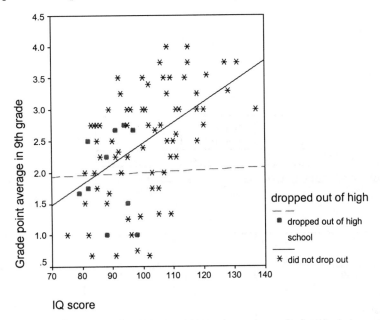

5.4   A sample scatterplot follows. It appears that both instructor knowledge and teaching skill are positively correlated with fairness of the exam.

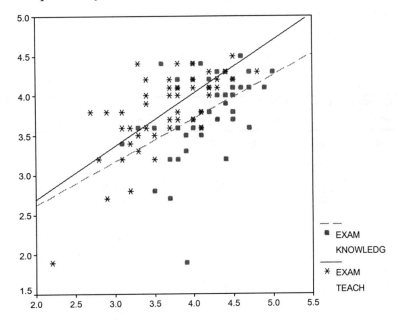

Exercises-Chapter 6

6.1   The regression output follows.

Model Summary

Model	R	R Square	Adjusted R Square	Std. Error of the Estimate
1	.301[a]	.090	.072	.59

a. Predictors: (Constant), GRADE

ANOVA[b]

Model		Sum of Squares	df	Mean Square	F	Sig.
1	Regression	1.669	1	1.669	4.775	.034[a]
	Residual	16.776	48	.350		
	Total	18.445	49			

a. Predictors: (Constant), GRADE

b. Dependent Variable: OVERALL

Coefficients[a]

Model		Unstandardized Coefficients		Standardized Coefficients	t	Sig.
		B	Std. Error	Beta		
1	(Constant)	1.718	.843		2.038	.047
	GRADE	.526	.241	.301	2.185	.034

a. Dependent Variable: OVERALL

6.2 A sample of the predicted values and residuals follows. They are the last 2 columns.

	overall	teach	exam	knowledg	grade	enroll	predover	resover
1	3	4	4	5	4	21	3.56	-.16
2	3	3	3	4	3	50	3.40	-.50
3	3	2	2	4	3	800	3.19	-.59
4	4	4	4	4	3	221	3.45	.35
5	3	3	3	4	3	7	3.40	-.40
6	3	3	4	4	3	108	3.40	-.90
7	4	4	4	5	4	54	3.61	.29
8	4	4	4	5	4	99	3.82	.48
9	4	4	4	4	3	51	3.29	.51

6.3 The regression output follows. It is consistent with the output in Table 11.6 of the textbook.

Model Summary

Model	R	R Square	Adjusted R Square	Std. Error of the Estimate
1	.813[a]	.661	.653	13.98

a. Predictors: (Constant), HEIGHT, SEX

ANOVA[b]

Model		Sum of Squares	df	Mean Square	F	Sig.
1	Regression	33886.657	2	16943.328	86.678	.000[a]
	Residual	17397.213	89	195.474		
	Total	51283.870	91			

a. Predictors: (Constant), HEIGHT, SEX
b. Dependent Variable: WEIGHT

Coefficients[a]

Model		Unstandardized Coefficients		Standardized Coefficients	t	Sig.
		B	Std. Error	Beta		
1	(Constant)	-88.199	43.777		-2.015	.047
	SEX	-14.700	4.290	-.302	-3.426	.001
	HEIGHT	3.691	.572	.569	6.450	.000

a. Dependent Variable: WEIGHT

6.4   The regression output follows. These results are consistent with those presented in Table 11.7 in the textbook.

Model Summary

Model	R	R Square	Adjusted R Square	Std. Error of the Estimate
1	.659[a]	.435	.411	7.66

a. Predictors: (Constant), BLAMBEH, DISTRES1, BLAMPER

ANOVA[b]

Model		Sum of Squares	df	Mean Square	F	Sig.
1	Regression	3161.406	3	1053.802	17.959	.000[a]
	Residual	4107.581	70	58.680		
	Total	7268.986	73			

a. Predictors: (Constant), BLAMBEH, DISTRES1, BLAMPER

b. Dependent Variable: DISTRES2

Coefficients[a]

Model		Unstandardized Coefficients		Standardized Coefficients	t	Sig.
		B	Std. Error	Beta		
1	(Constant)	14.052	5.782		2.430	.018
	DISTRES1	.640	.103	.564	6.184	.000
	BLAMPER	2.451	1.048	.247	2.338	.022
	BLAMBEH	.272	.990	.029	.275	.784

a. Dependent Variable: DISTRES2

Exercises-Chapter 7

7.1   The output from a single sample t-test follow. They suggest that students who did not read the passage got more answers correct than you would expect by chance, consistent with the conclusion drawn in the textbook.

One-Sample Statistics

	N	Mean	Std. Deviation	Std. Error Mean
score in no passage group	28	46.57	6.83	1.29

One-Sample Test

	Test Value = 20					
					95% Confidence Interval of the Difference	
	t	df	Sig. (2-tailed)	Mean Difference	Lower	Upper
score in no passage group	20.591	27	.000	26.57	23.92	29.22

7.2   The output follows. They are consistent with the results in the textbook.

Paired Samples Statistics

		Mean	N	Std. Deviation	Std. Error Mean
Pair 1	ELEVATE	1.4820	10	.3742	.1183
	LEVEL	1.4630	10	.3407	.1077

Paired Samples Correlations

		N	Correlation	Sig.
Pair 1	ELEVATE & LEVEL	10	.931	.000

Paired Samples Test

		Paired Differences							
					95% Confidence Interval of the Difference				
		Mean	Std. Deviation	Std. Error Mean	Lower	Upper	t	df	Sig. (2-tailed)
Pair 1	ELEVATE - LEVEL	1.9E-02	.1371	4.337E-02	-7.91E-02	.1171	.438	9	.672

129

7.3   A sample bar graph follows.

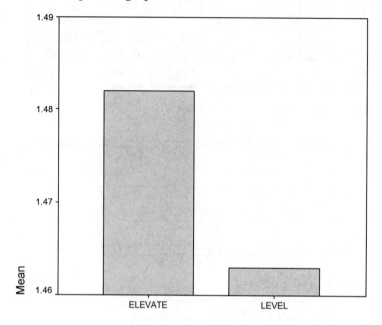

7.4   A boxplot follows. It is similar to the one in the textbook in Figure 14.3.

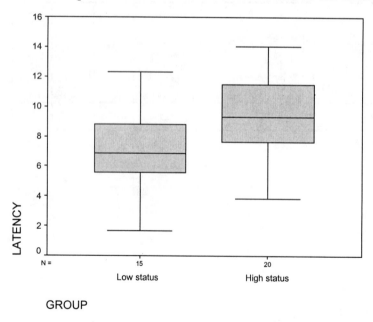

7.5   The output follows. The results are consistent with the textbook except that our t is positive. Either way, the difference between the 2 groups is statistically significant.

Group Statistics

		N	Mean	Std. Deviation	Std. Error Mean
	GROUP				
weight gain	family therapy	17	7.26	7.16	1.74
	control group	26	-.45	7.99	1.57

Independent Samples Test

		Levene's Test for	t-test for Equality of Means				
		F	t	df	Sig. (2-tailed)	Mean Difference	Std. Error Difference
weight gain	Equal variances assumed	.557	1.676	53	.100	3.46	2.06
	Equal variances not assumed		1.668	50.971	.101	3.46	2.07

7.6   The t-tests follow. After making all 3 possible comparisons, it seems that the family therapy group is the one that is most effective because it is the only one for which weight gain was significantly higher than the control group.

T-Test

Group Statistics

		N	Mean	Std. Deviation	Std. Error Mean
	GROUP				
weight gain	cognitive therapy	29	3.01	7.31	1.36
	family therapy	17	7.26	7.16	1.74

Independent Samples Test

		Levene's Test for Equality of Variances		t-test for Equality of Means				
		F	Sig.	t	df	Sig. (2-tailed)	Mean Difference	Std. Error Difference
weight gain	Equal variances assumed	.016	.898	-1.922	44	.061	-4.26	2.22
	Equal variances not assumed			-1.932	34.229	.062	-4.26	2.20

T-Test

Group Statistics

	GROUP	N	Mean	Std. Deviation	Std. Error Mean
weight gain	cognitive therapy	29	3.01	7.31	1.36
	control group	26	-.45	7.99	1.57

Independent Samples Test

		Levene's Test for Equality of Variances		t-test for Equality of Means				
		F	Sig.	t	df	Sig. (2-tailed)	Mean Difference	Std. Error Difference
weight gain	Equal variances assumed	.557	.459	1.676	53	.100	3.46	2.06
	Equal variances not assumed			1.668	50.971	.101	3.46	2.07

7.7   A sample bar graph follows.

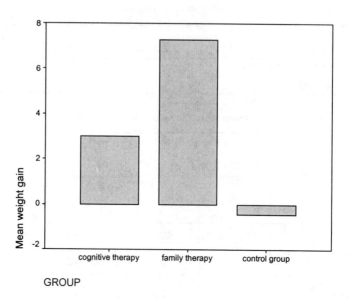

GROUP

132

Exercises-Chapter 8

8.1   The results follow. They indicate that there is a significant difference in recall based on condition. Specifically, people in the counting and rhyming conditions had significantly lower recall than all other groups.

ANOVA

RECALL

	Sum of Squares	df	Mean Square	F	Sig.
Between Groups	351.520	4	87.880	9.085	.000
Within Groups	435.300	45	9.673		
Total	786.820	49			

Post Hoc Tests

Multiple Comparisons

Dependent Variable: RECALL

LSD

(I) GROUP	(J) GROUP	Mean Difference (I-J)	Std. Error	Sig.	95% Confidence Interval Lower Bound	Upper Bound
Counting	Rhyming	1.00E-01	1.39	.943	-2.70	2.90
	Adjective	-4.00*	1.39	.006	-6.80	-1.20
	Imagery	-6.40*	1.39	.000	-9.20	-3.60
	Intentional	-5.00*	1.39	.001	-7.80	-2.20
Rhyming	Counting	-1.00E-01	1.39	.943	-2.90	2.70
	Adjective	-4.10*	1.39	.005	-6.90	-1.30
	Imagery	-6.50*	1.39	.000	-9.30	-3.70
	Intentional	-5.10*	1.39	.001	-7.90	-2.30
Adjective	Counting	4.00*	1.39	.006	1.20	6.80
	Rhyming	4.10*	1.39	.005	1.30	6.90
	Imagery	-2.40	1.39	.091	-5.20	.40
	Intentional	-1.00	1.39	.476	-3.80	1.80
Imagery	Counting	6.40*	1.39	.000	3.60	9.20
	Rhyming	6.50*	1.39	.000	3.70	9.30
	Adjective	2.40	1.39	.091	-.40	5.20
	Intentional	1.40	1.39	.320	-1.40	4.20
Intentional	Counting	5.00*	1.39	.001	2.20	7.80
	Rhyming	5.10*	1.39	.001	2.30	7.90
	Adjective	1.00	1.39	.476	-1.80	3.80
	Imagery	-1.40	1.39	.320	-4.20	1.40

*. The mean difference is significant at the .05 level.

8.2 An edited ANOVA summary table follows.

ANOVA

RECALL

	Sum of Squares	df	Mean Square	F	Sig.
Between Groups	351.520	4	87.880	9.085	.000
Within Groups	435.300	45	9.673		
Total	786.820	49			

8.3 I calculated eta squared through Analyze/Compare Means/Means. I could have calculated it also through General Linear Model/Univariate.

Measures of Association

	Eta	Eta Squared
RECALL * GROUP	.668	.447

8.4 A sample bar chart follows.

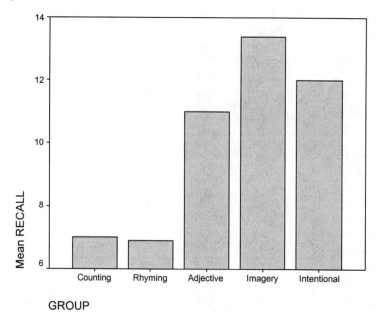

Exercises-Chapter 9

9.1   The output follows. You need to calculate your own F values by dividing the mean square for groups by the mean square error from the original analysis (8.026). When you do so, the F values are: .16, .31, 9.00, 10.99, and 33.20, for counting, rhyming, adjective, imagery and intentions respectively consistent with the values reported in the textbook.

CONDITIO = Counting

ANOVA[a]

RECALL

	Sum of Squares	df	Mean Square	F	Sig.
Between Groups	1.250	1	1.250	.464	.504
Within Groups	48.500	18	2.694		
Total	49.750	19			

a. CONDITIO = Counting

CONDITIO = Rhyming

ANOVA[a]

RECALL

	Sum of Squares	df	Mean Square	F	Sig.
Between Groups	2.450	1	2.450	.586	.454
Within Groups	75.300	18	4.183		
Total	77.750	19			

a. CONDITIO = Rhyming

CONDITIO = Adjective

ANOVA^a

RECALL

	Sum of Squares	df	Mean Square	F	Sig.
Between Groups	72.200	1	72.200	7.848	.012
Within Groups	165.600	18	9.200		
Total	237.800	19			

a. CONDITIO = Adjective

CONDITIO = Imagery

ANOVA^a

RECALL

	Sum of Squares	df	Mean Square	F	Sig.
Between Groups	88.200	1	88.200	6.539	.020
Within Groups	242.800	18	13.489		
Total	331.000	19			

a. CONDITIO = Imagery

CONDITIO = Intentional

ANOVA^a

RECALL

	Sum of Squares	df	Mean Square	F	Sig.
Between Groups	266.450	1	266.450	25.229	.000
Within Groups	190.100	18	10.561		
Total	456.550	19			

a. CONDITIO = Intentional

9.2 The output follows. These results are consistent with those in the textbook.

Tests of Between-Subjects Effects

Dependent Variable: maternal role adaptation

Source	Type III Sum of Squares	df	Mean Square	F	Sig.
Corrected Model	210.854[a]	5	42.171	3.984	.005
Intercept	12707.521	1	12707.521	1200.373	.000
GROUP	122.792	2	61.396	5.800	.006
EDUCATIO	67.688	1	67.688	6.394	.015
GROUP * EDUCATIO	20.375	2	10.188	.962	.390
Error	444.625	42	10.586		
Total	13363.000	48			
Corrected Total	655.479	47			

a. R Squared = .322 (Adjusted R Squared = .241)

9.3 A sample graph follows.

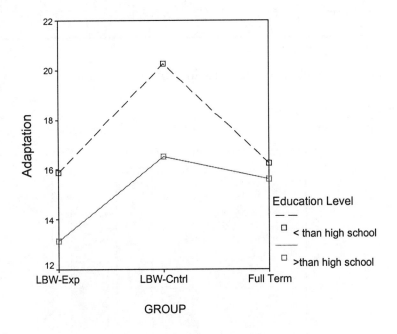

Exercises-Chapter 10

10.1   The within subjects output follows. The results are consistent with the textbook

Tests of Within-Subjects Effects

Measure: MEASURE_1

Source		Type III Sum of Squares	df	Mean Square	F	Sig.	Eta Squared
FACTOR1	Sphericity Assumed	351.520	4	87.880	20.218	.000	.692
	Greenhouse-Geisser	351.520	2.051	171.394	20.218	.000	.692
	Huynh-Feldt	351.520	2.664	131.972	20.218	.000	.692
	Lower-bound	351.520	1.000	351.520	20.218	.001	.692
Error(FACTOR1)	Sphericity Assumed	156.480	36	4.347			
	Greenhouse-Geisser	156.480	18.459	8.477			
	Huynh-Feldt	156.480	23.972	6.528			
	Lower-bound	156.480	9.000	17.387			

10.2   Eta squared is included in the previous output.

10.3   A sample graph follows.

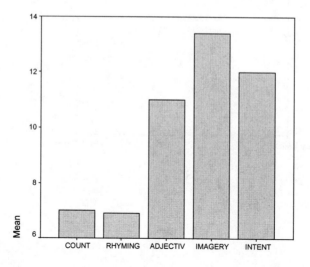

138

10.4   I calculated the new variable, lowproc. Then, I used a paired t-test to compare recall in the imagery and lowproc conditions. I did this because I knew it would calculate the mean difference for me. Then, I used the protected t-test explained in the text using the MS_{error} from the original analysis (see answer to exercise 1). The resulting t-value is 3.82, which is statistically significant with 9 df. Thus, recall was better in the imagery group than in the lower processing conditions.

Paired Samples Statistics

		Mean	N	Std. Deviation	Std. Error Mean
Pair 1	IMAGERY	13.40	10	4.50	1.42
	LOWPROC	9.2250	10	2.1745	.6876

Paired Samples Test

		Paired Differences					Sig. (2-tailed)
		Mean	Std. Deviation	Std. Error Mean	t	df	
Pair 1	IMAGERY - LOWPROC	4.1750	3.2017	1.0125	4.124	9	.003

Exercises-Chapter 11

11.1   The output follow. They are consistent with the data in the text.

ALLEY

	Observed N	Expected N	Residual
A	4	8.0	-4.0
B	5	8.0	-3.0
C	8	8.0	.0
D	15	8.0	7.0
Total	32		

Test Statistics

	ALLEY
Chi-Square[a]	9.250
df	3
Asymp. Sig.	.026

a. 0 cells (.0%) have expected frequencies less than 5. The minimum expected cell frequency is 8.0.

11.2   The output follows. The results support the hypothesis.

RATING

	Observed N	Expected N	Residual
not at all like me	8	5.0	3.0
somewhat unlike me	10	10.0	.0
neither like me or unlike me	20	20.0	.0
somewhat like me	8	10.0	-2.0
very much like me	4	5.0	-1.0
Total	50		

Test Statistics

	RATING
Chi-Square[a]	2.400
df	4
Asymp. Sig.	.663

a. 0 cells (.0%) have expected frequencies less than 5. The minimum expected cell frequency is 5.0.

11.3   A sample data file follows.

	bystande	assist	counts
1	.00	yes	11.00
2	1.00	yes	16.00
3	4.00	yes	4.00
4	.00	no	2.00
5	1.00	no	10.00
6	4.00	no	9.00

11.4   The results follow. They are consistent with the textbook.

BYSTANDE * ASSIST Crosstabulation

			ASSIST		
			yes	no	Total
BYSTANDE	.00	Count	11	2	13
		Expected Count	7.8	5.3	13.0
	1.00	Count	16	10	26
		Expected Count	15.5	10.5	26.0
	4.00	Count	4	9	13
		Expected Count	7.8	5.3	13.0
Total		Count	31	21	52
		Expected Count	31.0	21.0	52.0

Chi-Square Tests

	Value	df	Asymp. Sig. (2-sided)
Pearson Chi-Square	7.908[a]	2	.019
Likelihood Ratio	8.295	2	.016
Linear-by-Linear Association	7.321	1	.007
N of Valid Cases	52		

a. 0 cells (.0%) have expected count less than 5. The minimum expected count is 5.25.

Exercises-Chapter 12

12.1   The output follows. The z score is the same as the text, but the Ws are different. In both cases, the results suggest that there is a significant difference between groups. (Note: SPSS chooses to work with the sum of the scores in the *larger* group (71), and thus n_1 and n_2 are reversed. This will give you the same z score, with the sign reversed. Notice that z in the output agrees with z in the text.)

Ranks

	GROUP	N	Mean Rank	Sum of Ranks
BIRTHWEI	1	10	7.10	71.00
	2	8	12.50	100.00
	Total	18		

	BIRTHWEI
Mann-Whitney U	16.000
Wilcoxon W	71.000
Z	-2.132
Asymp. Sig. (2-tailed)	.033
Exact Sig. [2*(1-tailed Sig.)]	.034 [a]

a. Not corrected for ties.

b. Grouping Variable: GROUP

12.2   The output follows. There appears to be a significant increase in weight over the course of family therapy.

Wilcoxon Signed Ranks Test

Ranks

		N	Mean Rank	Sum of Ranks
weight after family therapy - weight before family therapy	Negative Ranks	4[a]	2.75	11.00
	Positive Ranks	13[b]	10.92	142.00
	Ties	0[c]		
	Total	17		

a. weight after family therapy < weight before family therapy

b. weight after family therapy > weight before family therapy

c. weight before family therapy = weight after family therapy

Test Statistics[b]

	weight after family therapy - weight before family therapy
Z	-3.101[a]
Asymp. Sig. (2-tailed)	.002

a. Based on negative ranks.

b. Wilcoxon Signed Ranks Test

12.3   The output follows. There is a significant difference in adaptation based on group.

Kruskal-Wallis Test

Ranks

	GROUP	N	Mean Rank
maternal role adaptation (low sores better)	LBW Experimental	29	40.17
	LBW Control	27	60.83
	Full-term	37	42.26
	Total	93	

Test Statistics[a,b]

	maternal role adaptation (low sores better)
Chi-Square	10.189
df	2
Asymp. Sig.	.006

a. Kruskal Wallis Test

b. Grouping Variable: GROUP

12.4   The output follows. There is a significant difference in recall based on condition.

Friedman Test

Ranks

	Mean Rank
COUNT	1.55
RHYMING	1.50
ADJECTIV	3.70
IMAGERY	4.35
INTENT	3.90

Test Statistics[a]

N	10
Chi-Square	31.474
df	4
Asymp. Sig.	.000

a. Friedman Test

annmablell@hotmail.com
250-619-2062 (cell).